A Look at Some of the World's Largest Churches

Compiled by

Dr. Alton E. Loveless

Cover picture:
New Creation Church
Singapore

Copyright 2015

By

Dr. Alton E. Loveless

ISBN 978-1-940609-39-3 Soft cover

FWB Publications
Enchanted Acres
1006 Rayme Drive
Columbus, Ohio 43207

FWB

ACKNOWLEDGEMENTS

It is impossible to list all the sources used to compile the information is this book. Google, Wikipedia, Wiki, Church websites, Denominational resources, etc. to whom I give thanks for the enlightenment of the growth of His Kingdom.

Introduction

Some say that America is in a post-Christian era, and perhaps it is. Whatever the case the church in America is stagnant, if not losing ground.

However, we have many large churches in America and many pastors are enamored with how they become as large as they have.

A **megachurch** is an American term for a Protestant church having 2,000 or more people in average weekend attendance and generating upwards of $25,000 in television coverage annually. The Hartford Institute's database lists more than 1,300 such Protestant churches in the United States; according to that data, approximately 50 churches on the list have average attendance exceeding 10,000, with the highest recorded at 47,000 in average attendance. While 3,000 individual Catholic parishes (churches) have 2,000 or more attendants for an average Sunday Mass, these churches are not seen as part of the megachurch movement.

Globally, 313 large congregations are a significant development in Protestant Christianity. In the United States, the phenomenon has more than quadrupled in the past two decades. It has since spread worldwide. In 2007, five of the ten largest Protestant churches were in South Korea. The largest megachurch in the United States is Lakewood Church in Houston, Texas with more than 40,000 members every weekend and the current largest megachurch in the world is South Korea's Yoido Full Gospel Church, an Assemblies of God church, with more than 830,000 members as of 2007 with 1,000,000 in 2015.

My research does not include all of these churches due to task and space and other's because of my inability to translate their website language or their available information.

For many years I have been involved in Christian education and have even authored a few books on the subject, but recently I started to investigate the largest churches in the United States and found that many of them have roots from other countries. Therefore, my interest changed from United States churches to the research of churches in various parts of the world and their growth. I divided them into various geographic regions believing that culture might have something to do with the church's growth. In my amazement, I found that the Christian movement is advancing much more rapid in foreign countries than they are in the United States of America.

C. Peter Wagner, in an article titled 'Those Amazing Post-Denominational Churches' wrote: "By far, the most rapidly growing segment of Christianity on all six continents is a type of church that does not fit traditional categories or classifications. Missiologists have recognized its presence for some time, but it is such a recent phenomenon that they have not yet agreed on a name for it. Perhaps one title that would fit is the term 'post-denominational.

The intention of this book is not to discourage but rather to enlighten what the church is doing around the world.

Largest megachurches
Average weekly attendances are shown in parentheses
1. Yoido Full Gospel Church, Seoul, South Korea (253,000)
2. Jotabeche Methodist P. Church, Santiago, Chile (150,000)
3. Calvary Temple, Hyderabad, India (120,000)
4. Deeper Life Bible Church, Lagos, Nigeria (120,000)
5. Elim Church, San Salvador, El Salvador (117,000)
6. Nambu Full Gospel, Seoul, South Korea (110,000)
7. AOG Grace and Truth, Kyanggi-do, South Korea (105,000)
8. Kum Ran Methodist, Seoul, South Korea (80,000)
9. Vision de Futuro, Santa Fe, Argentina (70,000)
10. Ondas del Luz, Buenos Aires, Argentina (70,000)
11. Young Nak Presbyterian Church, South Korea (60,000)
12. Winners Chapel, Ota, Nigeria (50,000)
13. Soong Eui Methodist, Inchon, South Korea (47,000)
14. Lakewood Church, Houston, Texas (45,000)

The cities in the world with the most megachurches are:
Seoul, Korea with 17; Nairobi, Kenya 12; Hong Kong, China 11; Lagos, Nigeria 10; Singapore 9; Abuja, Nigeria 7; London, England 6; Boondahng, Korea 5; Johannesburg, South Africa 5; Rio De Janerio, Brazil 5; Guatemala City, Guatemala City 4; Harare, Zimbabwe 4; Beijing, China 4; Kampala, Uganda 4; Accra, Ghana 3;Kiev, Ukraine 3;Manila, Philippines 3; Melbourne, Australia 3; Shanghai, China 3, etc.

The COUNTRIES in the world with the most megachurches are: Korea with 38; China 25; Nigeria 25; Australia 15; United Kingdom 14; Singapore 14; Kenya 13; India 11; Philippines 10; Indonesia 9; South Africa 9; Uganda 6; Ukraine 5; Zimbabwe 4, etc.

Denomination affiliation follows: 130 were non-denominational Charismatic, 35 Assembly of God, 21 Baptist, 20 Presbyterian, 6 Methodist, 4 Anglican, 3 Church of the Nazarene, 3 Evangelical Free, 1 Four Square Gospel, 1 Free Methodist and 1 Mennonite.

In the United States we look at the church from an American culture and from an affluent society. Most of the World's largest churches exist in huge cities where the latest technology is as common there and they use every available media to them.

The average age of these pastors is around 52 and the age of most church not relatively old.

Marvel with me and how those churches are movers and shakers in their society.

Blessings, Alton

Table of Contents

Africa

The continent of Africa has 71 churches in 13 countries with memberships that will range from 120,000 members down to 2000. There are 31 churches that range between 75,000 and 10,000. The country of Nigeria has 21 churches with Kenya as a close follower with 13 churches that fit in these mega-church categories. The countries are Nigeria, Kenya, Congo, Zimbabwe, South Africa, Uganda, Ivory Coast, Ghana, Rwanda, Egypt, Ethiopia, Burkina Faso and Zambia

Deeper Christian Life Ministry
Nigeria
120,000

Also known as **Deep in 13 different countries, Deeper Life Bible Church** is a non-denominational Christian Church with its international headquarters in Lagos, Nigeria. It is overseen by the General Superintendent of Deeper Life Bible Church, Pastor William Folorunso Kumuyi. It is a Holiness-Pentecostal church with an emphasis on holy living.

DLBC's website maintains a set of testimonials from people who claim supernatural healings have occurred as a result of prayers being offered by Pastor Kumuyi. These claims include the reversal of paralysis, spontaneous growth of limbs, spontaneous disappearance of mental diseases, and such.

The church teaches a doctrine of holiness and living a practical Christian life. The most important teaching of the church pertains to its members living holy lives. The General Superintendent, Pastor Kumuyi almost always during all his preaching's exhort members and newcomers alike to be born again so as to be qualified for the kingdom of heaven.

The Deeper Life Bible Church has branches in its home Nigeria and other countries, and is also known internationally for its strict adherence to the teachings of Christ, his apostles, and obedience to the word of God. The church lists 22 tenets of their beliefs: the holy Bible, the Godhead, Virgin birth of Christ, total depravity, Repentance, Restitution, Justification, Water baptism, Lord's supper, Sanctification, Holy Ghost baptism, Redemption, Personal evangelism, Marriage, Rapture, Resurrection of the Dead, Great Tribulation, Second coming of Christ, Christ's millennial reign, Great White Throne Judgment, New Heaven and the New Earth, and Hell fire.

History

In 1973, while serving as a Mathematics Lecturer at the University of Lagos, W.F. Kumuyi started a Bible study group with 15 university students who had come to him requesting training in the Scriptures. The church started as the Deeper Christian Life Ministry. William Folorunso Kumuyi, was a former Anglican who joined the Apostolic Faith Church after receiving the baptism of the Holy Spirit. In 1975, he was expelled from that church for preaching without being credentialed. He continued his independent ministry, which in 1982 became the Deeper Life Bible Church. By the early 1980s that small group had grown to several thousand, at which time Deeper Life Bible Church was formally established. The church has spread throughout sub-Saharan Africa and then to the United Kingdom, from where branches were developed in Western Europe, Russia, India, and North America.

By 1988 the congregation had grown to 50,000, and now numbers 120,000 members, and is considered one of the largest churches in sub-Saharan Africa, with a sizeable population in the world. Dr. Johan Combrinck reports that the Deeper Life Church not only has an attendance of 120,000 every Sunday, but has planted over 500 churches in Lagos, 5,000 in the rest of Nigeria (with an independent estimate of more than 800,000 members in Nigeria alone), and 3,000 elsewhere (with missionaries to 40 countries of Africa) as the movement missionary contribution.]

C. Peter Wagner, in an article titled 'Those Amazing Post-Denominational Churches' wrote: "By far, the most rapidly growing segment of Christianity on all six continents is a type of church that does not fit traditional categories or classifications. Missiologists have recognized its presence for some time, but it is such a recent phenomenon that they have not yet agreed on a name for it. Perhaps one title that would fit is the term 'post-denominational

"Go to almost any metropolitan area and ask to visit the largest Christian Church. Chances are it will be one of these new post-denominational churches'. In Lagos, Nigeria, it would be the Deeper Life Bible Church, pastored by William Kumuyi. On a recent Sunday I saw 74,000 adults worshipping together, with 40,000 children meeting in a separate building across the street"

On August 7, 2012, a Deeper Life church in Okene was attacked by three unidentified gunmen, who opened fire on a Bible study group with Kalashnikov assault rifles, killing 19.

In April 2013, Pastor Kumuyi was named as one of the "500 most powerful people on the planet" by the Foreign Policy Magazine.

Welcome by the pastor on their website

Dearly beloved,

I am delighted to warmly welcome you to our homepage. You have come to the right place at the right time. Here, we are very passionate about your eternal destiny and committed to your spiritual welfare. This is a website that has a lot to offer you – with unlimited access to life-transforming, systematic and expository teaching of the word of God and resources specifically tailored to meet your own spiritual needs; deepen your walk with God and add value to your entire life.

Our numerous resources are carefully prepared with you in mind- to satisfy your spiritual hunger; enhance your spiritual growth and; equip you for divine service, all round success and victory over the challenges of life.

You can now plunge into the great riches of the Kingdom that have been preserved for you via the hyperlinks to pages on downloadable sermons, Bible studies, target-group resources, gospel literature and magazines, leadership and church growth materials and faith-building testimonies etc. You can equally link up with us via this site for live streaming/broadcast of our regular refreshing worship and study sessions as well as soul-stirring, power-packed special revival services.

It is now my greatest delight to invite you to commit the rest of your life to the Great Saviour, Jesus Christ, who died for our sins-to accept Him as your personal Lord and Saviour; to enjoy the warmth of our fellowship, and then travel along with us on this highway of holiness to our eternal home in heaven.

Once again, I welcome you to a lifetime of unforgettable and eternally-beneficial experience of walking with God.

As you continue to explore and enjoy the riches of grace uncovered through our numerous materials and online resources, may the LORD continue to richly bless you (Amen). – Pastor W. F. Kumuyi.

Jesus Celebration Centre

Kenya
60,000

It is an incorporated ministry of the Redeemed Gospel Churches Inc. Redeemed Gospel Church was founded in 1974. By the current Presiding Bishop – Bishop Dr. Arthur Kitonga. Pushed by the desire of touching the lives and meeting people's needs, he established an independent Pentecostal Church (Redeemed Gospel Church) in Mathare Valley - Nairobi. The church adopted evangelism, blended with social concern, as a wholistic approach for the total man – body, soul and spirit – to meet the needs of the Valley community. Over the years, Redeemed Gospel Church Inc has spread its wings over the entire Eastern Africa and beyond and has a total of over 1000 branches locally.

The Lord had in his heart to do a work in the Islamic City of Mombasa that would rise beyond the boundaries and into international level to touch the Nations of the earth.

In 1983   Redeemed Gospel Church opened a church in Mombasa. After a brief period the then Pastor of the newly opened church relocated and Pastor Wilfred Lai was then appointed to take over the church which had a membership of about 60 members. In 1986 a vision was born that would take about three years without much happening physically but the Lord was preparing a great work of revival. This revival brought forth what is known both locally and internationally as JCC – Jesus Celebration Centre.

God gave His servant Dr. Lai a vision of Mombasa city saturated with the Gospel of Christ. People of all colors gathered with hands lifted high in Worship. At that time, the city was predominantly Moslem. Dr. Lai started his bold and aggressive declaration of this vision. At first this did not make sense to his critics and many of them called him a dreamer. Now past the nineties and into 2008, what then looked like a dream has become a reality and a complete marvel to many.   For all this we give God the glory.

Jesus Celebration Centre has grown from a humble beginning of 60 members to the great ministry that it is today with a membership of over 15,000.   God has raised JCC as a pioneer ministry in the nation of Nairobi and has been pace setter to many ministries in such areas as, Pioneered interdenominational lunch time services, JCC pioneered Television ministry in 1992, Pioneered Morning glory services, Pioneered unhindered dynamic praise and worship which has become a norm of ministry in many churches now.

JCC is founded on these main pillars:-

1.   Prayer
2.   Unhindered Praise
3.   Dynamic teaching and preaching of the
       Uncompromised Word of God
4.   Fellowship
5.   Evangelism

Over the years, the ministry has not lost grip of these pillars.

Since 1986 Pastor Augustus Lyimo was part of Jesus Celebration Centre (JCC) Mombasa Kenya under Pastor Wilfred Lai, where he was actively involved with praise and worship, hospital ministry and outreach ministry.

From 1991 to 1993 Augustino (Al) was in Tanzania under Bishop Emmanuel Lazarus of Tanzania Assemblies of God who had been working with Morris Cerulo actively involved in outreach. This music outreach covered all of Tanzania. During that period Augustino was assigned to help in a church, which due to difficult circumstances, had gone down in it's membership from about 250 members to 40. Within six to seven months the church had grown to about 180 to 200 members. This was a testing but fruitful experience for Pastor Augustino and the church.

In 1994 by the inspiration of the Lord, Augustino went back to Kenya where he planted a church in Ruwai, within 7 to 8 months it grew to about 175 members. Pastor Augustino committed the leadership into the hands of a pastor who had working with him in the ministry and he returned to pastor at JCC Mombasa under Wilfred Lai.

JCC Mombasa then released Augustino to come to the UK to attend the School of ministry at Kingdom Faith Bible Collage under Colin Urquhart. During that time he met his wife, married and moved to South Wales. In Wales Augustino undertook further studies at Learning Journey Elim Bible College. After completing his 4year education, the college sent Augustino to various churches to help.

In 1999 Pastor Augustino took his family back to Tanzania Arusha, where he started Zion Courts of Praise, which was and still is part of JCC Mombasa. He left the ministry with another pastor who was working under him in 2001 after hearing the call of God to come back to UK. Augustino attached himself with Life International Christian Fellowship (LICF) as part of international Co-ordinator, co-coordinating international meetings at the church, helping run the church and got involved in helping other ministries which came to seek assistance in LICF. One ministry in Luton which was at its dying stage, after three months saw revival as God worked through Pastor Augustino and the ministry was established with their own place and solid members.

In 2005 Pastor Augustino established JCC UK which is part of the mother church JCC Mombasa and will also serve as the Headquarter for Europe brunches.

VISION

To establish leadership training centers in all continents and plant churches in every city of the world so as to impact all the nations with the true Gospel of our Lord Jesus Christ

MISSION

To fulfill the great commission by making disciples in all Nations of the world who will be able to train others also. 2 Timothy 2:2

CORE VALUES

- Love
- Holiness
- Integrity

- Excellence
- Unity
- Diligence
- Creativity
-
- Before the Lord Jesus went to heaven, He called His disciples together and gave them a command. He commanded them not to leave Jerusalem until they are endowed with power from heaven.(Acts 1:3). The work that they were given to do was an impossible task without the help of the God. Therefore they needed to be filled with the Holy Spirit who would help them to accomplish this great task. Jesus told them that after they receive the Holy Spirit, they will have power to be His witnesses beginning in Jerusalem, to Judea and to Samaria and to the uttermost parts of the earth. (Acts 1:8.) It is very important to understand that their mission could not be fulfilled without the help of the Holy Spirit. The Holy Spirit was going to give them the ability to do the works that Jesus did; to preach the gospel of the Kingdom of God,to heal the sick and to cast out demons. This work that they were given is commonly known as the Great commission.

- The great commission was given to the disciples of Jesus but it has become the mission of the church. In the commission they were commanded to go into all the world and make disciples of all nations.(Mathew 28:17-20 and Mark 16:15-17). The task was too great for them and therefore it has been passed over from one generation to another. The generation that will fulfill it will be the one that will see the closing of the age or the end of the world. Jesus told them that this gospel of the kingdom shall be preached to every creature for a testimony and then the end will come. (Matthew 24: 14).

- So what is a great commission cell?

- *It is a small group of disciples who gather together to learn how to win souls and disciple them to become disciples also.*

Living Faith Church Winners Chapel

Nigeria
50,000

Our Mandate speaks of liberation in all facets of human existence, we focus mainly on destinies that have been afflicted, battered, beaten, tattered, deformed and subsequently in groaning and agonies, as a result of pains, pangs and crying. This is the mandate.

"The hour has come to liberate the world from all oppressions of the devil through the preaching of the word of faith, and I am sending you to undertake this task."

Today, testimonies of liberation through our messages, books, tapes, magazines and other periodicals are most humbling. The word of faith is working like fire for the liberation of mankind across the nations.

David O. Oyedepo (born September 27, 1954) is a Nigerian Christian author, preacher, the founder and presiding Bishop of Living Faith Church World Wide, also known as Winners' Chapel, and its affiliated international churches known as Winners Chapel International, with headquarters in Ota, Ogun State, Nigeria. Oyedepo is the senior pastor of Faith Tabernacle, a 50,000 seat church auditorium, reported to be the largest church auditorium in the world by the Guinness Book of Records.[1]

The Winners' Chapel network of churches is located in over 300 cities, in all states of Nigeria, as well as, in several cities in 45 African nations, Dubai, the United Kingdom and the United States. Oyedepo has been seen as one of the pioneers of the Christian charismatic movement in Africa and has been referred to as one of the most powerful preachers in Nigeria. He is the Chancellor of Covenant University and Landmark University. He was named in 2011 by *Forbes* magazine as being the richest pastor in Nigeria.

On September 27, 1954 David Olaniyi Oyedepo was born in Osogbo, Nigeria, but is a native of Omu-Aran, Kwara State, Nigeria. He was raised in a mixed religious family His father, Ibrahim, was a Muslim healer. His mother, Dorcas, was a member of the Eternal Order of the Cherubim and Seraphim Movement (C&S), a branch of the Aladura movement in Nigeria. He was raised by his grandmother in Osogbo, who introduced him to the virtues of Christian life via early morning prayers which she attended with him. She also taught him the importance of tithing.

Oyedepo was born again in 1969, through the influence of his teacher, Betty Lasher, who took special interest in him during his high school days. He studied architecture at the former Kwara State Polytechnic, now Kwara State University and worked briefly with the Federal Ministry of Housing in Ilorin before resigning to concentrate on missionary work. Oyedepo received a Ph.D. in Human Development from Honolulu University, Hawaii, United States.

Oyedepo claimed to have received a mandate from God through an 18-hour vision in May 1981, to liberate the world from all oppression of the devil through the preaching of the word of faith. This is the inaugural vision that led to the founding of the Living Faith Church World Wide (LFCWW), first called Liberation Faith Hour Ministries, in 1981. Two years later, on September 17, 1983, Pastor Enoch Adeboye, General Overseer of the Redeemed Christian Church of God, ordained David and his wife, Florence Abiola Akano (known as Faith Abiola Oyedepo) to become pastors and officially commissioned the new church. Five years later, Oyedepo was ordained as Bishop.

Living Faith Church (AKA Winners Chapel) started in Kaduna but moved to Lagos, the former capital of Nigeria in July 1989, to start a new branch of the church after Oyedepo claimed to have received instructions from God to reach out to the people of Lagos.

Publishing Mandate

The word of God came to His servant Bishop David Oyedepo, saying:

"The Word I have put in your mouth, the same commit to writing and I will cause the unction on the spoken word to rest upon the written word, producing the same effect."

For more than two decades, Dr. David O. Oyedepo, has been part of the current charismatic renaissance overwhelming the world. His faith-based teaching has impacted millions of lives.

Called with a specific mandate to liberate mankind from all oppression, Dr. Oyedepo is the Presiding Bishop of Living

Faith Church Worldwide a.k.a Winners Chapel (World Mission Agency) with a network of churches all over Nigeria and most nations of Africa, Europe and USA.

"We are not publishing for money, we are publishing to make men stop mourning!

We owe the people education, and this is what we are doing with the word of faith in prints... it is a ministry of illumination by literature." -Dr. David .O. Oyedepo

As an educationist, his mission currently pioneers the establishment of educational institutions at all levels in Nigeria including the recently established Covenant University, and Landmark University where he serves as the chancellor.

Oyedepo claimed to have received a mandate from God through an 18-hour vision in May 1981, to liberate the world from all oppression of the devil through the preaching of the word of faith. This is the inaugural vision that led to the founding of the Living Faith Church World

Oyedepo is the wealthiest preacher in Nigeria with a net worth of over USD $150 million. The church owns four private jets and several buildings around the world, including London and the United States. Oyedepo is an author and publisher who has written over 70 titles apart from periodicals. He is the Chairman/Publisher of Dominion Publishing House (DPH), a publishing arm of the ministry. DPH has over 4 million prints in circulation to date. Through Oyedepo Covenant University, Faith Academy and Kingdom Heritage Schools have been established to equip the youth for global impact. The construction of a third university named Crown University is already underway, located in Calabar, Cross Rivers, Nigeria.

Place of Worship

Bishop Oyedepo claims that in 1998 he was instructed by God to build a new base for the Commission to accommodate the increasing number of worshippers. This resulted in Bishop Oyedepo's church's acquisition of the initial 530-acre (2.1 km^2) facility, known as Canaanland, which serves as the headquarters. It is the home of the 50,000-seat capacity auditorium, the 'Faith Tabernacle', which is reputed to be the largest church auditorium in the world. This was a feat also recorded by the Guinness Book of Records.

Construction was completed within 12 months. Reports also claimed that this building was built debt free. This 50,000-seat edifice was dedicated on September 18, 1999

under the administration of former President Olusegun Obasanjo.

Canaanland is in Ota, Ogun state and is the 5,000-acre estate and campus, that houses the 50,000 church building, the church secretariat, the church's youth chapel, a primary school called Kingdom heritage model school, a full boarding mission secondary school called Faith Academy, with over 1,500 students and the Covenant University facilities, which accommodates over 7,000 students, fully resident in ultra-modern hostel facilities, with fully equipped faculty buildings and numerous staff housing facilities. Canaanland campus also has for profit establishments operated by the church such as a bakery, a bottled water processing plant, a petrol station, various restaurants and shopping stores, several residential houses that provide for the over 2,000 church employees, and guest houses. Four banks are also present on this Estate, three of which are branches of external commercial banks and one which is a community and micro-finance Bank and operated by the Church. The whole of Canaanland which includes a proposed 15,000 housing estate known as Canaan City had increased to 17,000 acres as at 2012.

Christian ministry

The teachings of Oyedepo has put him in the category of what is commonly called the Word of Faith Movement. He has referred to principal exponents of the Faith Movement such as Kenneth Copeland, Gloria Copeland, the late Kenneth Hagin, E. W. Kenyon, T. L. Osborn, Smith Wigglesworth as well as renowned Nigerian preachers Enoch Adeboye and the late Benson Idahosa as mentors.

His Winners Chapel operates a Bible training program known as Word of Faith Bible Institute for members and non-members alike to develop knowledge of Christian principles and to develop leaders and future pastors. This institute is run in major branches of the Church.

Oyedepo is the President of David Oyedepo Ministries International (DOMI). DOMI is the umbrella organization comprising Living Faith Church World Wide (a global network of churches), World Mission Agency (WMA); the global missionary arm of the church's operations, Dominion Publishing House; the publishing arm of the church, Covenant University, and the Social Development Missions projects (made up of hospitals, maternity homes, schools, etc.

Bishop David Oyedepo

WMA is making significant contributions to education in Nigeria. It established the Faith Academy in 1999, a model Christian college geared towards raising pupils with a testimony of academic excellence and spiritual prowess. The Academy's working team is made up of carefully selected, spirit-filled professional men and women of proven integrity and outstanding teaching, administrative and technical capabilities. Their overall objectives are to help each child discover his or her purpose, release their potential, nurture their latent abilities to become not only productive and fulfilled citizens but to be pacesetters in all areas of life. Currently, twenty more secondary schools have been established; of which are seven full boarding schools, Thirteen Day Schools and one day and boarding school. Two additional Faith Academy Day Secondary

Schools shall commence operation by September within Lagos Metropolis.

In addition to the above, the network of nursery and primary schools, called Kingdom Heritage Model Schools, were established from 2002 across the cities of Nigeria and some other African nations. The overall objectives are to help each child discover his or her purpose, release his/her potentials and nurture their latent abilities; to become not only productive fulfilled citizens, but to be pace-setters in all areas of life. Today, the KHMS are one hundred and forty seven (147) across thirty out of the thirty six states in Nigeria, and six in other African countries.

In 2002, World Mission Agency, in a graphic demonstration of its commitment to the provision of education at all levels, established Covenant University (CU). Of note is the fact that seasoned Christian intellectuals and professors with proven academic excellence and international acclaim make up the faculty of the University. The premises of Covenant University is an array of architectural master pieces consisting of the largest Centre for Learning Resources (university library), college buildings, a 3,000 seat capacity Student Chapel, Professors' Village, Staff quarters, Students Halls of residences, etc.

Since 2005, the University has been adjudged the best private university in Nigeria by the National Universities Commission (NUC), and has held that position till date. In addition to other distinctions and awards on the university, the Chancellor and the Vice Chancellor, the university has been named as NEPAD bioinformatics research center. In July 2006, Covenant University graduated its pioneer students, and continues to produce some of the world's best graduates. This is in line with the prophetic mandate of 1 of 10 in 10 by the year 2022.

A second University, the Landmark University (LMU), was added in 2011. A University with an agrarian mandate, in its few years of existence, has begun to make waves by becoming the second best private University in Nigeria. LMU has 3 colleges: Agricultural Science, Science & Engineering and Social Science & Business. The first set from these colleges graduated in 2014.

Landmark University runs a farm with large acres planted with crops, a big fishery and large poultry.

United Family International Church

Zimbabwe

35,000

The United Family International Ministries comprises of The United Family Interdenominational Ministries and The United Family International Church.

The Interdenominational Ministry is the mother ministry of the other ministries and arms which will fall under the United Family International Ministries.

The fellowship could only last for a week at the Anglican Cathedral due to limited space as numbers swelled by the day. After one week break, moved to The State Lotteries Hall.

Vision
Building a God society of all people of all nations.

Mission
To unite the body of Jesus Christ (the church) through catering for the less privileged members of the society (widows & orphans), reaching out for the poor and the broken hearted ultimately imparting revelation knowledge of Jesus Christ and

fellowshipping with God The Father, God The Son, and God The Holy Spirit.

Evangelism

The Interdenominational rolled out its Evangelism arm mid-2010 and started a week long crusade at Chitungwiza, Unit 'L' community grounds in May 2010. This event was to redefine 'ministry' from the stand point of the magnitude of the harvest. Over 5,000 people gave their lives to Christ with an amazing 1,190 doing it the first day, in which Prophet Makandiwa did not preach but just called an alter call of repentance unto salvation. This was to be followed by St. Marrys, Highfield and Muzarabani.

Prophet Makandiwa delved into his apostolic gift and planted churches around Harare and in Mashonaland Central. After mass baptisms these churches were officially opened and this was the birth of The United Family International Church.

Prophet Emmanuel Makandiwa was born in December 1977 into a family of small farmers. It is believed he grew up using the name Shingirai Chirume. His parents are elders in the Apostolic Faith Mission Church in Muzarabani district of Mashonaland Central Province. In 1993, Makandiwa and other boys of his age spent six months with the late pastor Mukwaira on "crusades". Makandiwa, after completing his secondary education at Zengeza High school in Chitungwiza, returned to help his parents till the land. In Muzarabani, Makandiwa started taking God's word seriously and the next four years turned his life around.

With his parents he organized gospel crusades and preached from home. In 1995, he was reportedly called in a vision by God to deliver his people from the bondage of Satan and teamed up with local AFM Pastor Rev. Munyengeterwa on gospel crusades. In 2000, Makandiwa enrolled at the AFM's Living Waters Theological Seminary in Harare, graduating in 2002.

After finishing his pastoral studies, Rev. Makandiwa chose to go to Matabeleland and worked as an assistant pastor under the supervision of Rev. Madzivire, who is now the president of AFM. "I started ministry in Bulawayo in 2003. When I moved to Harare in 2006 it was Evangelist Chiweshe who welcomed me into the province he was heading in Chitungwiza . And he gave me an assembly to pastor. As my overseer I could see his effective leadership style as he led by example. He could call me any time to lay his hands on me or give guidance. I would not hesitate to say that of all the men I have come across in Zimbabwe, here was the only man I can boldly declare was full of wisdom and exhibited a high level of maturity." echoed Prophet Makandiwa , as he was expressing how he felt over the death of Evangelist P. Chiweshe .

After ordination, he was given an assembly in Shangani where he became the talk of the neighborhood with his demonstrations of the power of God. In 2004, he was transferred to How Mine and subsequently to Hebron Assembly in Chitungwiza.

History

Prophet Makandiwa started his own Church, called United Family Interdenominational Ministries in August 2008. By then it was just more of a lunch hour fellowship and members would meet at the Anglican Cathedral, Cnr Sam Nujoma / Nelson Mandela. From the first day, the hall was filled to capacity (approximately 600 people) and by the following day the fellowship encountered an overflow as people swarmed from the Parliament side just to get a glimpse of proceedings. By the second day people would come as early for a lunch fellowship which only started at 1300 hrs . This phenomenon has stuck as a benchmark to date as people flock The City Sports Center.

Between 2009 and 2010, other vibrant Pastors within AFM also followed suit, and launched their own "fellowship" services, and this did not go down well with the supreme leadership of AFM, which is known and the AFM Apostolic Council. In early 2010, Makandiwa who was still a pastor by then, was suspended from Ministering at the AFM Hebron assembly (in Chitungwiza), after he failed to honor the Council's resolution that no pastor shall run or lead an interdenominational organization. This must have been the time when the Prophet went to Ghana to have a meeting with His Spiritual Father, Prophet Victor Boating, who inspired him and spiritually advised him on how to set up his own church. Upon his return from Ghana he began using the title "Prophet", since he was known as a Pastor during the time that he was with AFM.

There are also some who claim that his expulsion from the Apostolic Faith Mission (AFM) was a result of serious differences over the source of his "healing" powers, while other churches accuse him of "stealing their people". Always controversial, some men have gone so far as to accuse him of ruining their marriages by exposing their extra-marital affairs to their wives through his prophecies. His followers say these allegations are a result of jealousy. Some pastors and leaders of various churches have also questioned the origin of the power Prophet E Makandiwa uses to perform his miracles or prophecies, this was further worsened when the media competed in writing articles about Prophet Makandiwa soon after he launched his Spiritual Link Airtime Juice Cards in August 2011, a move that POTRAZ said could have violated the laws of the country.

In April 2011, Makandiwa led a National All Night Prayer at the National Sports Stadium, where he filled the 60,000 seater stadium with his followers from all parts of the nation. This was the fourth time the National Sports Stadium had been full to capacity since 1980, (the first time was during the 1980 Independence celebrations, second time was in 2010 when Zimbabwe played soccer against Brazil and the third time was also in 2010 when ZAOGA hosted its 50 years jubilee celebrations).

The greater part of Makandiwa's close buddies are well respected and recognized men of God. Chief among them are Apostle T Vutabwashe, who is the founder and head of Heartfelt Ministries. Their companion has been existing for years, Apostle Vutabwashe would host an annual "Catch the fire Revival Crusade" even when he was still pastoring in AFM and Makandiwa would often not always be invited as the most dynamic guest speaker. His other close friends include Prophet Uebert Angel, who is the founder and head of Spirit Embassy International and Bishop Albert Chikuni, who is the founder of Family Life Ministries International.

Prophet Makandiwa's church, United Family Interdenominational Church meets on Sundays at the City Sports Centre in Harare. They have since secured their own stand in Chitungwiza, where plans to start constructing their 30,000 seat church are at an advanced stage. The church, however, now has branches in almost every city, and they are still planting new branches in other cities and towns of the country.

Prophet E Makandiwa is well known for his powerful sermons, and his favorite area of preaching is the topic of Prosperity. He is also famous throughout the country and also in neighboring countries for his miracles and prophecies that have been confirmed to be true by a great number of people throughout the country. A number of people have been reportedly healed of various diseases including Cancer and HIV after receiving prayers from Prophet Makandiwa . He indeed is both one of the youngest universally known pastors from Zimbabwe, as well as one of the richest pastors in Zimbabwe. The setup of his services is almost so similar to that of Prophet T B Joshua of Nigeria. In fact, it has been mentioned a number of times that

Prophet T. B. Joshua is the Spiritual Father of Prophet Victor Boateng , and Prophet Boateng is the Spiritual Father of Prophet E Makandiwa.

Business Empire
United Family International Church (UFIC) founder Emmanuel Makandiwa owns a controlling stake in Zimbabwe Stock Exchange-listed Radar Holdings (Private) Limited (Radar) among other multi-million dollar businesses.

The popular prophet, who believes in the doctrine of hard work and servant leadership modelled along biblical greats such as King David, also owns a raft of businesses, including agricultural concerns.

As details of his private life emerge, the charismatic preacher who draws up to 50,000 congregants at his church services per week, also owns a huge stake in entertainment giant, Sterkinekor's franchise locally and in Zambia.

Such is the man's riches that Makandiwa is building a multi-million dollar house in Glen Lorne, which has often been mistaken for a hotel.

Prime Kufa, the UFIC leader's spokesperson, confirmed to the Daily News that indeed his boss was building a mansion touted as a "mission house for foreign dignitaries and visitors".

There have been allegations that Makandiwa could be using church funds to live a wealthy lifestyle where he can afford to build a huge mansion and drive top-of-the-range vehicles, but Kufa insisted that Makandiwa gets money from his huge businesses.

"When people hear that the man of God is doing A, B, C or D, all what comes to their minds is that there are church funds involved.

"If that was the case, how is it possible that the man of God is our biggest benefactor and the ministry owes him a lot of money?

"In that respect, we feel that as sons, we have also let him down by not divulging some of the man of God's sources to the public domain.

Pastor Makandiwa's home

"He is a man who believes his private life is just that — private!

Pastor with famed leader Mandela

"These are not just claims but information that can be accessed as it is available in the public domain. "That has always been his philosophy from long back and I remember him quoting for me from Acts 20:33-34," he said: "I coveted no man's silver or gold or costly garments. You yourselves know personally that these hands ministered to my own needs and those of the persons who were with me" (AMP) as he was teaching me why I should embark on projects as a pastor," Kufa added.

The spokesperson said it is folly for people to think that Makandiwa could single-handedly build a 30,000-seat church, look after nearly 2,000 orphans, 300-plus widows and be constantly donating houses with his only source of income being the church.

The close Makandiwa aide said "people ought to be fair to the man and not criticize him just because they do not understand him".

"If what he is doing for the church and community at large is not enough to qualify him to live the life that he lives, I do not know what will.

"For example if he has bought his assistants and pastors Mercedes Benz vehicles, given out more than 400 cars, is it too much if he drives a Mercedes Benz himself.

"Show me a man that is doing more for his community and I will gladly pledge to be praying for him every day of my life."

Word of Life Bible Church
Nigeria
30,000

Pastor Ayo Oritsejafor is a dynamic preacher. He is a Pastor, Evangelist, Teacher, Prophet, Apostle and an Author, with a unique anointing of God upon his life. In 1972, the Lord saved and miraculously delivered him during a crusade. Almost immediately, he felt the call of God upon his life and enrolled in the New Covenant Bible Institute, Benin City, Nigeria.

While in college the Lord showed him a vision of himself preaching to countless thousands of people with great power and authority and he heard the Lord say "Take my Word to the World".

His anointed messages have brought Salvation, Deliverance, Revival, Healing and outstanding Miracles to millions across the world as God's power is demonstrated with signs and wonders.

As a keynote speaker, he has ministered in crusades with well over 2,000,000 souls in attendance. He has also ministered and still ministers in various international and local Conferences and seminars which has taken him to well over 50 countries and every continent of the world.

In a bid to carry out God's divine mandate of bringing the message of Salvation, Deliverance, and Healing to the homes of countless millions, Pastor Ayo started a TV

program, (HOUR OF DELIVERANCE) in 1980. Currently, he's on several Cable Networks all over the world and preaching the word of God through the internet via this website.

As a prolific writer, he has authored several books amongst which are *"Walking in Unity"*, *"Power through The Church"*, *"The Battle is in the Mind"*, *"Be an Over-Comer"*, *" Power for the Journey"*, *"Faith Antidote For Daily Living"*, *"A Voice in the Wilderness "*, *"A Man amongst Men "* to mention but a few.

He is currently the national president, Pentecostal Fellowship of Nigeria (PFN) and president, Christian Association of Nigeria (CAN).

In view of the apostolic call upon Papa Ayo, his ministry acts as a covering to several ministries in Africa, Europe and America.

THE CHURCH

The International Gospel Center, Ajamimogha Warri. From a very humble beginning of using a class room to a warehouse and then an open field. Today, in a 35,000 Seat Church Auditorium, one of the largest in the world.

This structure can seat over 35,000 adults, 17,000 children and a conference center sitting over 5,000 people. This indeed is one of the biggest Church building in the world because it has actually sat over a 100,000 people during one crusade.

VALUES

- Integrity: Members are expected to show complete moral and ethical uprightness in their decisions and actions. II Cor. 8:21, Prov. 11:3, 20:7
- Accountability: It is expected that members should be responsible for their actions and inactions. Lk.16:2, Matt.16:27
- Leadership by Example: Leadership must transform and motivate. As role models, leaders at all levels should be absolutely transparent by doing the things they say or expect of others. Matt.16:27
- Initiative: Members must recognize their responsibilities to make things happen.Phil.3:13-14
- Growth and Development: Members must be involved in activities that would enable them to release their potentials and develop

their talents. I Pet.2:2 Eph.4:14-15, II Tim.4:14, I Tim.1:6.

- Service: The idea of making contributions continually shall be the mindset of members. Mark 10:45.
- Love: Members should show empathy and seek opportunity to do good to all men especially to them that are of the house hold of faith. Gal. 6:10, I John 3: 17-18.
- EQUITY: Members should at all times exhibit a high sense of trust and fair play in their interpersonal relations. Luke 6:31.

o **MEMBERSHIP:**

Word of Life bible church defines membership on the basis of Acts 2: 41-42 "...then they that gladly received his word were baptized... and they continued steadfastly in the Apostles doctrines and fellowship and in breaking of bread and in prayers".

Thus a member shall be one who believes in the Gospel. Baptized by the immersion. Attends teaching canter, Home Fellowship and meetings consistently. Faithful in paying His/Her tithes. Well known by leaders and brethren of the home fellowship with respect to type of business/Job engaged in and general life-style. Based on the above membership definition, anyone that falls short of this requirement would be referred to as a Nominal member

COMMON BELIEF:

o That the holy Bible consisting of 66 books is the inspired, authoritative and infallible word of God. II Tim.3:16-17.

- That the God-Head consists of three persons in one: The father, Son and the Holy Spirit. II Cor. 13-14.
- In repentance towards God. Acts 3:19.
- In justification and regeneration. John 3:3.
- In Restitution where possible. Luke 19:8-9.
- In Sanctification (Holiness). I Thess. 4:3.
- In baptism of the Holy Spirit with the evidence of speaking in tongues and in the gift of the Holy Spirit. Mk. 16:17-18.
- In water Baptism by Immersion. Acts 8:38, 39.
- In Divine Healing. Isaiah. 53:5.
- In the second coming of Jesus Christ as literal and visible as His First ascension to Heaven. Acts 1:9-11.
- In Eternal Heaven and eternal hell. Rev. 14:1-11.
- That the Lord's Supper should be observed by all believers in accordance with I Cor. 11:23-28.
- That excerpts where otherwise provided for in Scriptural marriage is binding for life. Matt. 11:9, I Cor.7:15.
- That tithing is a command to all believers. Mal. 3:7-10.

TEACHING CENTERS:

We operate a unique system of worship wherein we meet generally for service on Sunday only. The weekly services and other training are done in our respective teaching centers spread all over Delta state.

HOME FELLOWSHIP:

We operate a home fellowship system with a vision to establish about ten on every street in our city (Warri) and a total of ten thousand all over the state. We are on the move home fellowship centers are being established on a daily basis.

Pentecostal Churches in Zimbabwe

Pentecostal Churches in Zimbabwe are almost always evangelical in character (and so are sometimes called "Evangelical Pentecostal Churches"). Accordingly, most churches of Pentecostal character in Zimbabwe belong to the Evangelical Fellowship of Zimbabwe, was founded in 1962.

These churches typically emphasize the "African gifts of the spirit", including healing. The term "African Initiated Church" (AIC) is used of any of a number of Christian churches started in Africa by Africans and not directly by missionaries from another continent. Often they contrast themselves with the so-called missionary churches and emphasize traditional gender roles and social structures. Most Pentecostal churches (with the exception of the Apostolic Faith Mission and Celebration Church) fall into the AIC category.

A variety of overlapping terms exist for these forms of Christianity: African Initiated Churches, African Independent Churches, and African Instituted Churches. Note: *Religion in Zimbabwe* uses the term "African Indigenous Churches" for a separate group of churches which almost exclusively target Africans and are often concerned with local customs.

Some large Pentecostal churches or movements include:

- Apostolic Faith Mission in Zimbabwe
- Bethesda Apostolic Church
- Celebration Church
- Christ the Rock Ministries International

- Church Team Ministries International
- Elim Pentecostal Church
- Faith Ministries
- Full Gospel Church of God in Zimbabwe
- Gospel Assembly Church
- Grace Unlimited Ministries International
- Harvest House International Church
- Impact Christian Centre
- New Life Covenant Church
- River of Life International
- Spirit Embassy
- Tabernacle Pentecostals
- United Family International Ministries
- Zimbabwe Assemblies of God Africa (ZAOGA)

Apostolic Faith Mission in Zimbabwe

The Apostolic Faith Mission in Zimbabwe Church (AFM) is one of the largest Pentecostal denominations in Zimbabwe. Until independence in 1980, it was part of the Apostolic Faith Mission of South Africa, which is South Africa's largest Pentecostal church.

Faith Alive assembly is a church of the Apostolic Faith Mission (AFM) in Zimbabwe based in the Adylin section of Westgate in Harare. From humble beginnings with a congregation of less than 12 people, it has since grown to more than 1,300 people. AFM Faith Alive church building was officially opened on the 4th of July 2009 by the former President of AFM in Zimbabwe, Reverend Manyika, on a colorful occasion that was attended by believers from different churches, as well AFM leaders from Zimbabwe and South Africa.

See also Apostolic Faith Mission International and the Apostolic Faith Mission of Africa (Bulawayo), a branch of the Apostolic Faith Mission of Africa based in Masvingo.

Bethesda Apostolic Church

Bethesda Apostolic Church was founded in 1952 after Loveless Matarirano Manhango received numerous visions near Chegutu (formerly Hartley).

The women's fellowship, named Ruwadzano, wears a blue-red-white uniform revealed in a vision to the founder. The Church maintains a current website with numerous photos and downloads.

Celebration Church

Founded since Zimbabwean independence by Senior Pastors Tom and Bonnie Deuschle from America. Celebration Churches have created a wide network of ministries and enterprises with a contemporary media awareness. There Celebration Churches in Harare, Kadoma, Bulawayo, as well as South Africa.

Christ the Rock Ministries International

Christ the Rock Ministries International frequently organizes seminars and workshops that are aimed at equipping believers with competence in subjects to do with business and finance from a Christian perspective. It was established in 1998 and has churches in Australia, New Zealand, the United Kingdom, South Africa, Malawi, Zambia and Zimbabwe. CTRMI's Head ministry office is located in Harare, Zimbabwe.

Church Team Ministries International (CTMI)

After more than 20 years of working in the Indian Ocean Islands, Africa, Europe, India, and America, CTMI has united men and women from diverse cultural backgrounds who work together to equip and encourage church leaders. As a result, a growing network, made up of leaders and churches sharing the same vision, has been established in over 22 countries.

CTMI Countries : Botswana, Burundi, Cameroon, Congo Republic, DR Congo, France, India, Kenya, La Réunion, Malawi, Mauritius, Mozambique, Nigeria, Rodrigues, Rwanda, Seychelles, South Africa, Tanzania, Uganda, United Kingdom, USA, Zambia, Zimbabwe.

Elim Pentecostal Church

A local branch of the Elim Pentecostal Church founded in Ireland in 1915, Elim Zimbabwe runs a hospital, schools and over 50 churches. Elim is headed by Pastor Pious Munembe.

The Mutare Memorial church, which also houses the Headquarters of Elim Zimbabwe, was built with funds raised following the Vumba massacre. On 23 June 1978, twelve people were slaughtered at the Elim Mission station in the Vumba Mountains, northern Zimbabwe. The first Elim Missionaries to Zimbabwe were Mr and Mrs Jessie Williams who went in February 1949 and were based at Penhalonga, located north of Mutare.

Faith Ministries

Faith Ministries is a charismatic, Bible-based ministry with communities in Zimbabwe and the UK. It was started in 1976 by a Scotsman called Alastair Geddes.

Full Gospel Church of God in Zimbabwe

Through its amalgamation with the Church of God which is represented in 162 Countries, the Full Gospel Church of God in Southern Africa is an International Church. In the year 1909 George Bowie came to South Africa as a missionary sent from the Bethel Pentecostal Assembly, under the leadership of Minnie Draper, Newark in New Jersey, U.S.A It was in the month of April 1910 that the Pentecostal Mission was started, and this Pentecostal Mission was to become The Full Gospel Church of God in Southern Africa, a bilingual Church— in 1995 there were 82 congregations and 7,200 members; 14,400 people were affiliated with the church.

Gospel Assembly Church

Gospel Assembly Church is a non-denominational Pentecostal Church with branches all over the world. In Zimbabwe they have branches in all major cities of the country. Gospel Assembly Church Bulawayo is located in the suburb of Romney Park. The Bulawayo Assembly is pastored by Rev Eddie E. Gatsi with his wife, Joyce Gatsi.

Grace Unlimited Ministries International

Bishop Langton Kanyati and Bishop Florence Kanyati co-founded Zoe Life Changing Ministries and Grace Unlimited Ministry, which are active in Harare through teaching and healing crusades. Bishop Langton's publications include *Building a Great Home – Establishing a Strong Marriage*. Bishop Florence has also written a number of books on Christian marriage and her women's ministry is particularly visible.

Harvest House International Church

Harvest House International Church (HHI) is one of the leading Pentecostal Churches in Southern Africa. It has followers all over Zimbabwe. Outside the region, this Church has believers in Australia, Nigeria and England. Bulawayo community founded in October 1995 with just 8 people is, currently, building a 12,000-seater conference center for its rapidly-accelerating congregation.

Impact Christian Centre

Impact Christian Centre puts emphasis not only on praise and worship and teachings of the word of God, but also on achieving excellence by its members. The Impact Young Executives, is the Church's Youth Ministry where the ICC looks at how to groom youths to be ladies and gentlemen, as well as future leaders. ICC was founded in 2010 by Pastors Davison and Gwen Kanokanga.

New Life Covenant Church

Jubula New Life Covenant Church is a multi-ethnic Harare based congregation with a large number of cell groups with a leader and a stable cell host. The activities of its 26 churches around Zimbabwe include intercessory prayer, leadership development, economic empowerment, social engagement, evangelism. Bishop Tudor and Pastor ChiChi became the senior pastors of what was then New Life Temple in 1982. In the years since they have assembled a multi-ethnic, multi-cultural congregation. New Life Temple became New Life Covenant Church in 1998.

River of Life International

River of Life International is affiliated to the Faith Ministries family. River of Life was born on the 17th of December 1999.
After serving with Victory Fellowship under the leadership of the Apostle Kenneth Eric Haskins, Pastor and Prophet Bothwell Tiger Phiri left to fulfill the call of God to start the ministry.

Spirit Embassy

Spirit Embassy was founded by Prophet Uebert Angel on March 12, 2007. Spirit Embassy Church has 20 branches worldwide including cathedrals in South Africa, the United States of America, the United Kingdom and Zimbabwe.

Tabernacle Pentecostals (Branhamites)

The post-World War II faith-healing movement founded by William Branham has several congregations in Zimbawe including Spoken Word Tabernacle and Eastlea Tabernacle in Harare.

United Family International Ministries

United Family International Ministries (UFIM) comprises the United Family Interdenominational Ministries and The United Family International Church. It was founded by Prophet Emmanuel Makandiwa and operates mostly around Harare and in Mashonaland Central.

UFIM charity work in Chitugwiza.

This ministry is one of the fastest-growing in Zimbabwe, largely due to the charisma of their leader. According to the UFIM site, an estimated 17,000 people joined them in 2010 in a period of three months.

Launched in August 2008 as a lunch-hour fellowship at the Anglican Cathedral in Harare, the fellowship was so popular, that after only a week at the cathedral, it moved to the State Lotteries Hall and subsequently to the City Sports Centre.

Zimbabwe Assemblies of God Africa

Zimbabwe Assemblies of God Africa (ZAOGA) is a large Pentecostal church known internationally as Forward in

Faith Ministries International (FIFMI). As of 2000, there were 4,000 congregations and 539,683 members. ZAOGA is divided into 26 provinces in Zimbabwe. The movement was founded in the late 1950s by a group of Pentecostals from the Apostolic Faith Mission who gathered around the charismatic Ezekial H. Guti. He continues to lead the church and holds the titles of Dr., Apostle and Archbishop. Zimbabwe is the location of the ZAOGA-FIF headquarters and the host-nation of a number of international gatherings for FIFMI.

ZAOGA has schools in Zimbabwe including Grange Primary School in Chisipite, Denda Primary in Mutoko, Christ for Zimbabwe High School, a children's home in Mutare, as well as three bible schools in Harare, Chiredzi, and Bulawayo.

According to an article posted on ZAOGA-FIF website in May 2012, "In Waterfalls (a suburb of Harare) the church recently built a state of the art hospital. This medical institution also has a non-medical unit where those with spiritual needs will be ministered to through prayer and the Word."

The Zimbabwe Ezekiel Guti University (ZEGU) is currently under construction in Bindura on a 100 hectare property.

David Maxwell, in his book *African Gifts of the Spirit: Pentecostalism & the Rise of Zimbabwean Transnational Religious Movement,* traces the transformation of Ezekiel Guti and his prayer band from small beginnings into the present day transnational enterprise, which is now ZAOGA. See review of this book.

Asia

The area that we know is Asia has 131 churches that ranged from 420,000 members down to as low as 2000. They are found in 12 Asian countries with Korea representing with 38 churches that fall into this category. India Philippines Singapore and China average about 11 per country. The other countries that are represented are Sri Lanka, Malaysia, Iraq, Japan, Taiwan and Thailand. This area of the world has the largest number of churches that would exceed 35,000 in their membership.

Yoido Full Gospel Church - Seoul, Korea
Largest Church in the world with 420,000 members

There are big churches, and then there's the Yoido Full Gospel Church here in Seoul, South Korea. It's the mother of megachurches, with the largest congregation in the world. On a typical day 200,000 will attend one of seven services along with another two or three hundred thousand watching them on TV in adjoining buildings or satellite branches. While some other churches may be losing members, this one just keeps growing. The main sanctuary here holds 21,000 worshipers packed to the rafters seven times every Sunday. Each service has its own orchestra, its own choir, its own pastor. There are hundreds of assistants. Each service is translated into 16 different languages for visitors

1958 - 1961, The Early Years - the Tent Church

The founding of the Yoido Full Gospel Church can be dated back to May 18, 1958, when the first worship service was held with the attendance of Pastor Cho Yonggi and Pastor Choi Jashil, in the living room of Pastor Choi Jashil. The first service was more a home worship service than what many conceive as a Sunday worship service.

On the morning of the first service, Pastor Choi Jashil put together a pulpit by covering an apple box with a cloth, and went around the neighborhood announcing the service to be held. However, her efforts were in vain as the first service was attended by, other than Pastor Cho Yonggi and Pastor Choi Jashil, three of Pastor Choi Jashil's children and an elderly woman who had come in to escape being drenched by the rain.

About a month after that fateful day, Pastor Cho Yonggi and Pastor Choi Jashil happened to hear of a woman who had been paralyzed for the past seven years. This woman had suffered from paralysis during the birth of her son seven years earlier, and had never been able to stand on her own since then.

The moment the two pastors entered her residence, their lungs were filled with foul odor making it difficult for them to breathe. The children were uncared for and filthy beyond belief. Pastor Choi Jashil immediately embarked on washing and cleaning the woman and her children with water. Then with Pastor Cho Yonggi, they placed their hands on top of the woman and began praying in tongues. Pastor Cho Yonggi shouted from the top of his voice, "In the name of Jesus, you shall overcome your paralysis."

After several days of prayer and spiritual warfare, a miracle took place. The woman began grabbing on to the wall and slowly began to stand. Then, ever so slowly and carefully, she kicked up her feet and began to walk step by step. That day she was completely healed of her paralysis and began to take an interest in the church.

Such sweat-filled prayers and unwavering dedication of the two pastors began to bear fruit and the membership of the church increased to 50 at which time Pastor Choi Jashil's living room became no longer adequate to contain the worshippers. As a solution, a tent was pitched in the front yard of Pastor Choi Jashil's house, and with empty rice sacks serving as flooring, worship services were held. As time passed, the membership in the tent-church continued to grow, necessitating bigger tents to be pitched to accommodate the growth, all funded by the meager offerings of the congregation who mainly consisted of those who were in need themselves.

Beginning in the living room of Pastor Choi Jashil, the church experienced phenomenal growth as the work of the Holy Spirit was manifested in the church since the pitching of the first tent, making The first tent church symbolic of the now Yoido Full Gospel Church.

As many members of the congregation were healed through the power of the Holy Spirit and many others found solace and solutions to their problems, the church grew day by day. A paralytic patient for seven years recovered from the paralysis, and a shaman priestess repented of her sin and accepted Christ as Saviour. Many suffering illnesses were healed as they experienced the great power of the Holy Spirit. There were even thugs_members of local gangs, who repented and turned their lives toward God, becoming His servants. Day by day, the church grew.

In the 1950's however, especially toward the close of the decade, Korea's situation, both economically and politically, was not rosy by any means. It was not long after the Korean War and there were many suffering poverty and chaos from the war's aftermath. Pastor Cho Yonggi was no exception. It was not uncommon for Pastor Cho Yonggi to satisfy his hunger with nothing other than three meals of porridge given him by an American evangelist. He also battled poverty along with the members of his congregation. In such desperate times, Pastor Cho Yonggi called out to God for messages appropriate for such harsh reality.

One day as he was reading the Bible, he heard the voice of the Holy Spirit and the message of the Three-Fold Blessing (the blessing of the Spirit, the soul and the body). Filled with confidence and certainty, he delivered the message of faith which led the congregation to positive, creative and productive lives. His messages provided faith, hope and confidence to those suffering from despair and hopelessness. The promise of God driven by his intense faith in God, led the church to experience incredible growth in three years.

With the dawning of the New Year, 1961, Pastor Cho Yonggi and Pastor Choi Jashil were filled with exuberance and hope for the New Year. By then, the church had 1,000 registered members with 600 of them attending on Sundays.

Then the unexpected happened. Pastor Cho Yonggi received a draft notice from the army requiring him to honor mandatory service. This was a devastating blow to Pastor Cho Yonggi, as he had thought he would be exempt due to his ill health. It seemed as though all the plans he had made for the church crumbled much like a tower of sand under the weight of the draft notice. Pastor Cho Yonggi and Pastor Choi Jashil began fasting and praying every night for the will of God. About two or three days prior to the day of his enlistment, an unexpected visitor came to the church from Pusan, an American evangelist, Pastor J. W. Hurston. He told them he was irresistibly drawn by the voice of the Holy Spirit every time he prayed to visit the tent church. God had brought him from hundreds of kilometers away, a

Spirit-filled servant of God who would keep lit the fire of the Holy Spirit during Pastor Cho Yonggi's absence.

Having been comforted, Pastor Cho Yonggi entered into the army. After two months of boot camp, Pastor Cho Yonggi was fortunately assigned to an American army base near Seoul, allowing him to participate in the ministry of his church. However, in the spring of 1961, as Pastor Cho Yonggi was baptizing the members of the church, the accumulation of overwork and exhaustion caused him to collapse in the middle of the service.

1962 - 1972, The Church at Seo - Dae - Mun

After undergoing a major operation and discharge from the army, the church entered into a new phase of growth.

Not long after his discharge from the army, on September 1, 1961, a great tent crusade was held at the Seo-dae-mun interchange on the field where a circus was often held. Sam Todd was the preacher for the crusade, and Pastor Cho Yonggi provided the interpretation.

The crusade drew people from all over Seoul, and they gathered at the crusade much like the gathering of rain clouds. Not to mention the scores of souls who accepted Jesus Christ that day, many of the sick were touched by the healing hand of the Holy Spirit. During the period of the crusade, Pastors Cho Yonggi and Pastor Choi Jashil made a decision to establish a church at Seo-dae-mun.

On October 15, 1961, a church was established at the very place where the crusade had taken place and the first worship service was held. It was named the Full Gospel Revival Center. However, a problem, legal in nature, forced the Full Gospel Revival Center to acquire the help of an attorney, "Hwang Sung-su", and his expertise. His wise and dedicated counsel made the completion of the church a reality the following year.

On April 26, 1962, Pastor Cho Yonggi received pastoral ordination. On May 13th, the Full Gospel Revival center was renamed, the Full Gospel Central Church. By then, the church membership had grown to over 500.

Three years later, by 1964, the Seo-dae-mun church grew to a membership of 3,000. In the same year, Pastor Cho Yonggi was invited to attend the 50th anniversary celebration of the American Assemblies of God, and He left on his first trip abroad. He attended the celebration as the one representing Korea, and having delivered a sermon in English, he did a splendid job of introducing Korea to all in attendance.

On March 1, 1965, Pastor Cho Yonggi entered into holy matrimony with the daughter of Pastor Choi Jashil. Pastor Cho Yonggi's marriage to Grace Kim was a culmination of Pastor Choi Jashil's 10 years of praying. With the blessing of the then 3,000 members of the church, Pastor Cho Yonggi walked down the aisle with Grace Kim.

The Full Gospel Central Church continued to grow to a membership of 5,000, then 6,000, then 7,000. By 1968, the church had 8,000 members, necessitating three services to be held on Sundays. Even with three services on Sundays, those who came late to the services were not able to find seats within the church, but were required to sit in the parking lot on plastic mats as they listened to the worship service over the loudspeakers. Having to lead three worship services, Pastor Cho Yonggi continued his battle against exhaustion and overwork, delivering his messages with fervor and perspiration as he had always done.

With the continued growth of the church, Pastor Cho Yonggi was also required to lead the baptismal services even more often. One day, as he was baptising several hundred people, he once again succumbed to overwork and exhaustion, and collapsed to the floor. As he was recovering in the hospital, the hospital doctor recommended Pastor Cho Yonggi change his profession. Brushing aside the doctor's advice, Pastor Cho Yonggi discharged himself from the hospital to deliver the Sunday messages.

As he went forward to the pulpit, however he dropped unconscious to the floor and was forced to return the hospital once again. Then a wondrous thing happened as Pastor Cho Yonggi began to read the Bible from Genesis on. As he was reading in Exodus, a particular verse, Exodus 18:18 moved his heart.

"You and these people who come to you will only wear yourselves out. The work is too heavy for you; you cannot handle it alone."

The next morning, Pastor Cho Yonggi called a meeting with the elders and deacons to share with them the wisdom he had received from God through the Bible. This was the birth of the cell system.

Although the elders and deacons realized the function and the necessity of the cell system, they were not yet trained to be able to implement the idea. Pastor Cho Yonggi realized that there was a need for a training program for those who would become cell and district leaders.

As Pastor Cho Yonggi continued to search for solutions for the training of those who would be leaders, he learned another fact: that the men were reluctant to make home visits to other members. He realized that for this purpose, women were much more suited than the men.

At the time, Korean society frowned upon women taking the role of leaders within groups containing both men and women.

Even so, as the Holy Spirit moved the hearts of both men and women, such social obstacles were overcome and women played a critical role in the development and growth of the YFGC.

The home visits by the cell leaders proved to be an effective method in drawing the new members into the fold of the church. And with the continued wok of the Holy Spirit, these cells and the cell system worked effectively to promote fellowship between the members of the cells and the districts.

In 1967, when the cell system was introduced, it consisted of 7,750 individuals of 2,267 families organized into 125 cells.

Currently, YFGC has adopted the district system to better help all members of the church.

On a weekly basis, district members consisting of district leaders, the elders, the deacons and deaconesses, and lay members gather together for meetings to further promote the growth of the church.

Aside from the implementation of the cell system, in 1960, the women's Fellowship Association was formed. In 1963, the men's Fellowship Association was added. These two organizations currently play a central role in volunteer services which make possible the various services held by the church.

In 1967, to further aid the qualitative, spiritual growth of the members and also to spread the Holy Spirit movement, the monthly "Faith" magazine was first published. It was an evangelical tool for the purpose of spreading the Holy Spirit movement based on the Word of God. The monthly periodical contained God's messages, testimonials, and Bible studies for the purpose of education and evangelism. From its first issue, the quality and the reach of the monthly periodical continued to expand, extending all across the southern peninsula.

1. The Growing Church

The membership of the church at Seo-dae-mun continued to skyrocket day by day. With the membership reaching 10,000, the Seo-dae-mun church was no longer adequate to accomodate all the members. Accordingly, the church began looking for a new place to build. Although many places were considered, it was not easy to find the right place to build a new church to accommodate its continuing growth.

It was then that Yoido was submitted as a candidate. At the time, Yoido Island was undeveloped and was being used as a runway for aircraft. Being a desolate island at the time, there was not even a bridge to connect it to the city of Seoul. It was obvious that one of the problems for the congregation would be the means of travel to the island. However, through much prayer by Pastor Cho Yonggi, he was assured that Yoido was indeed the place which God had prepared. With this answer from God, a piece of land was purchased in Yoido. Having purchased the land, the problem of funds necessary to build a church became a hurdle. The great amount of funds required seemed an unsurmountable obstacle. However, Pastor Cho Yonggi who believed in the miracle of God forged ahead with his burning desire to build a church in Yoido.

From the laying of its foundation, the church faced many difficulties, including the immediate problem of securing the funds. Coinciding with the Middle Eastern "oil shock", the exchange rate of the Korean won to the dollar plummeted, sending the cost of building material to a new high. Added to this external negative factor, the church also faced a drop in tithe income.

Many of the members of the church lost their jobs as a result of the "oil shock", and the banks which had loaned the funds to the church lowered the credit rating of the church, causing the debt repayment to be a heavier burden on the church. As the pressure increased, the construction of the church came to a halt, a truly devastating situation. Pastor Cho Yonggi began going out to the construction site, grabbed hold of the bare iron bars which stood like the skeletons of the building, and began praying to God nightly. "Oh God my Lord! It would be better if these bars fell on me and released me from this turmoil." Rain or shine, Pastor Cho Yonggi kneeled on the empty rice sacks and cried out to the Lord.

One by one, those who shared faith in God's plan and providence began joining Pastor Cho for the nightly prayers. With the passage of time, the prayers to save the church began to build momentum. Then, one member brought to Pastor Cho Yonggi the proceeds from the sale of his gold and jewelry possessions. This became an impetus for other members to also offer the church the proceeds from the sales of what they had sold. Such faith, love and devotion to God and the church made it possible to repay the debts and complete the YFGC.

The first worship service at the now YFGC was held on August 19th, 1973. On September 18-22, 1973, the 10th Pentecostal World Conference was held at YFGC and the Hyo-chang Stadium with 50,000 Koreans and 5,000 foreign guests in attendance. On September 23, the inaugural worship service of thanks was held at the church with 18,000 church members in attendance. With this service, YFGC entered into a new era.

Following the relocation to Yoido, the church in 1977 grew to a membership of 50,000 persons, a mere four years after the completion of the church. The growth continued and reached 100,000 by 1979. Along with the numerical growth in number, the church also began to transform in other ways, including further expansion. On January 20, 1977, the 10-story world Evangelical Center (currently the First Education Building) made its appearance. Then on December 31, 1981, the 13-story Second Education Building was built. This building also contained a television studio which handled the broadcast of the worship services both domestically and internationally.

750,000 Members
Yoido Full Gospel Church

In March of 1973, the O-san-ri Prayer Mountain in memory of Pastor Choi Jashil was founded. Since then, many Christians have come to Prayer Mountain to fast and pray, receiving the Holy Spirit and experience Divine Healing as well as finding solutions to their individual and personal problems. This prayer mountain was named the "O-san-ri Choi Jashil Prayer Mountain" to honor Pastor Choi Jashill who had devoted her life to the founding and the growth of the YFGC from its very inception. Currently, along with the main sanctuary which was completed on July 4, 1982, there are countless numbers of private prayer rooms and 12 other smaller sanctuaries.

Two years following the growth of the church to a membership of 100,000 on November 4, 1979, the church grew to a number of 200,144 members on November 30, 1981. To celebrate such wondrous growth, a special worship service was held inviting Mr. Daemus Shakarian, the president of American Full Gospel Association of Business Owners. The L.A. Times reported on the growth of the church to 200,000 members and emphasized the YFGC as the largest church in the world.

With the growth to 200,000 members, Pastor Cho Yonggi began to establish independent churches around the country. One important point to note is that all such independent churches which were established eventually became the largest churches in their areas. This was not only true for the churches which were established domestically, but also for the churches which were established abroad. The servants of God who were sent out by YFGC or the foreign pastors who attended the C.G.I (Church Growth International) conferences all were blessed greatly by God and experienced a wondrous growth in their churches.

Having reached 200,000 members, the growth of the church never stopped but continued until the membership reached 400,000 by October of 1984, making YFGC the fastest growing church in the world. The growth continued to 500,000 in 1985, and to 700,000 in 1992. Even though Regional Chapels began to be established in the early 1980s throughout Seoul's many districts and wards, becoming independent churches with certain freedom of autonomous control draining the membership of YFGC continued to grow to 700,000, which testifies to the work of the Holy Spirit.

In the 1980s, after the establishment and the inaugural service in 1973, YFGC entered into a phase of reconstruction to enlarge the capacity of the church. With the completion of the building expansion in May of 1986 of YFGC which had begun on January 22, 1983, the church was able to accommodate 25,000 individuals for each service. In

November of 1984, the 33-meter monument of a cross and praying hands was built in front of the main sanctuary, and in 1985, the sculptured external wall of the church's facade was added.

In September of 1992, Pastor Cho Yonggi was elected as the chairman of the Executive Committee of the World Pentecostal Assemblies of God Fellowship now known as the World Assemblies of God Fellowship which had a membership of 30,000,000 members among 60 nations of the world. The election took place at the 16th Pentecostal World Conference which was held in Norway from September 9th to 13th, 1992. Up to that time, the Assemblies of God were in the control of the American leadership, but with the election of Pastor Cho Yonggi, the main impetus of the Holy Spirit movement was passed on to Korea.

A religious periodical in America, the Christian World, placed YFGC as the first among the "50 Great Churches of the World." Along with this honor, YFGC was honored as the church with the largest congregation in the world by the Guinness Book of World Records, and a ceremony was held at the Hilton Hotel Convention Center to commemorate YFGC entering the Guinness Book of World Records.

The Full Gospel Educational Research Institute was established to educate lay members and to promote Full Gospel theology. It was renamed the Young-san Research Institute in August of 1990. In March of 1993, it expanded again and became the International Theological Institute, a specialized theological research institute. ITI was founded to further develop and promote Full Gospel theology and adopted the motto, "Think deeper, wider and forward," and actively supports the dispatch of evangelists both educationally and financially, it became an "assistant" to Pastor Cho Yonggi's ministry of evangelism.

In March of 1996, a collection of Pastor Cho Yonggi's sermons were printed. The 21-volume series was published throughly the Seoul Logos Company, and it contained the messages which Pastor Cho Yonggi delivered during his 40 year ministry. A night of honoring Pastor Cho Yonggi's publication of the collection of sermons was held at the Crystal Ballroom of the Lotte Hotel on the night of March 14th. The function was attended by former Deputy Prime Minister Han Wan-sang, former Prime Minister Chung Keun-mo, the Chancellor of Yonsei University Song Ja and other notable figures of Christianity in Korea.

2. The Church Reaching Out to the World

The establishment of the Full Gospel American Mission Association in March of 1976 provided Pastor Cho Yonggi with an opportunity to spread the Gospel throughout the world. In April of the same year, the European Mission Association was formed, followed by the Japanese Mission Association in August of that year.

In September of 1977, the Full Gospel Central Church built a Full Gospel Theological Seminary in the United States, in the city of Los Angeles, in West Germany's city of Berlin in July of 1977, in the city of New York in February of 1978, in Kobe, Japan in April of 1978, and in the city of Chicago in

April of 1980. The aim of the theological schools was the nurturing of those who would serve God. Then in August of 1980, a Graduate School of Theology was built in California.

Since taking the first step toward world evangelization in September of 1964, Pastor Cho Yonggi has ceaselessly striven and continued to devote his efforts toward world evangelization. In January of 1981, Pastor Cho Yonggi was invited to the congratulatory celebration of the Inauguration of the 40th president of America, Ronald Reagan, and was honored to deliver the message. The honor of doing so confirmed Pastor Cho Yonggi's establishment as a truly internationally recognized pastor.

Not only has Pastor Cho Yonggi gone out in person to evangelize, he has also invited many foreign servants of God and church leaders to provide them with an opportunity to learn about church growth through direct experience and study. On November 4th of 1976, for the promotion of church growth, a research department was established and was given the name CGI. Since its birth, CGI has held over 250 seminars attended by 6,800,000 people from throughout the world. As such, CGI has taken the role of leadership in promoting the growth of churches all across the world.

Meanwhile, YFGC also continued its focus toward world evangelization through countless publications of sermon collections, recorded messages on tapes, and broadcasts of worship services. Domestically, Pastor Cho Yonggi's Friday, Saturday, and Sunday messages were broadcast regularly through the MBC affiliate broadcast stations in Taejeon,

Kwang-ju, Jun-joo and Masan. Internationally, Pastor Cho Yonggi's sermons were carried through the broadcast stations in Los Angeles, CBS in New York, and through the Gingki and Sun Broadcast stations in Japan.

In addition to the 12 domestic radio stations which send out Pastor Cho Yonggi's sermons through the airwaves, Pastor Cho Yonggi's sermons were carried through the radio airwaves in New York, Dallas, Houston, and Washington.

In 1994 during the 1st World Assemblies of God Fellowship Congress, a grand prayer rally was held on October 3 at Yoido Square. Throughout the world, 30,000,000 Christians from 25 countries simultaneously participated in this grand prayer rally. On the day of the world prayer rally, over a million Christians gathered in Yoido Square necessitating a simultaneous interpretation of the messages in Japanese, Chinese, Spanish, and Indonesian, Swedish, and English.

On February 7, 1996, the 2,000 Jerusalem Celebration was held at the birth place of our Jesus Christ, Jerusalem. The celebration memorialized the coming of Christ 2000 years ago and also the reign of King David 3000 years ago. From 31 countries around the world, 5000 Christians came to celebrate the event.

Since July 28, 1996, through the use of the first Korean artificial satellite, the "Mu-keung-wha," YFGC has been providing a satellite broadcast of the worship services for not only the affiliate churches in Korea, but also to the churches in Japan and other parts of Asia. This has made it possible for church members throughout Korea and Asia to participate in the Sunday and Wednesday worship services simultaneously, paving the road for greater promotion of the Five-fold Gospel and Three-fold Blessing both in Korea and internationally.

As the world entered the 90s and with the advent and widespread use of high speed, high capacity personal computers, YFGC has not remained behind but has taken active steps to utilize the new communication tool, the internet. "We shall cover the world with the message of the Full Gospel," has become the motto of the Full Gospel Internet Broadcast Station which was launched on December 24, 1998. With its establishment, Christians throughout the world are able to easily access information and the Gospel provided by YFGC.

3. The Church for the People

On October 3, 1987, the Prayer Crusade for the Nation and the People mobilized over one million people at the Yoido Square notwithstanding the fact that the Crusade coincided with a national holiday, and proved to be a truly blessed event for all who attended. After the close of the crusade, with Pastor Cho Yonggi taking the lead and one million gatherers including those who organized the crusade, the mass of people marched in an orderly manner toward City Hall, singing hymns of praise to the Lord and chanting for peace. After the crusade, all offerings given on that day were donated to charity to help orphaned children live alone on their own.

On July 26, 1988, the Elim Welfare Town, the biggest such welfare facility in Asia, was completed to help orphaned children or those suffering from extreme poverty, and the citizens who had nowhere to turn. The YFGC, which had the ideal of putting Christian love to practice, ceaselessly provided welfare services to those in need. In 1987, the governmental department of Social Welfare officially recognized Elim Welfare Organization of the YFGC as a welfare institute. The same year, with the support of 15 billion won from YFGC, Elim Welfare Town was built. Elim Welfare Town covers a vast land area, the largest for any welfare institution in Asia, and has the capacity to accommodate 500 orphaned children providing them with job training, as well as 200 senior citizens.

On behalf of the document mission and the Gospelization of the Korean people, the Kookmin Daily Newspaper was established on December 10, 1988. The Kookmin Daily is the world's first daily periodical with the emphasis on the Christian mind and ethics. Also, as it was the voice of 12 million Christians in Korea, it opened a new chapter in evangelism through mass-communication. From its very founding, the Kookmin Daily has helped the needy of the society, shared their pain and suffering, and taken an active role in various drives such as the Aid for Young Men and Women, the Aid for Africa, the Blood Collection Drive, and the National Kindness Campaign.

YFGC also actively practices Christian love by collecting donations to provide free surgical aid to children who suffer heart-related diseases. On April 1, 1993, the charity work of the church was recognized and YFGC received a plaque of appreciation from the Office of Kyonggi Province. YFGC also had the honor of receiving the award of highest honor at "The 1st Environmental Awareness" on January 23, 1995, sponsored by the Korean Christian Environmental Awareness Coalition.

Emeritus Pastor Cho

Pastor Cho was born on 14th February, 1936 in Southern part of Kyongsang Province, Woolju Town, Sam-nam Kyodong village. He was born from his father, Cho Doo Cheon, and mother, Kim Bok Sun as the first born of 5 brothers and 4 sisters. He learned a lot from his father who was very knowledgeable in Chinese, Confucianism, and Buddhism.

Fortunately, there was an American Military Camp near-by the school that he could learn English from American soldiers. So he occasionally translated in between the school principal and the Military Camp Commander.

However, when he was 17 years old, he was diagnosed with pulmonary tuberculosis and had only a short period of time to live.

Yet he still ignited the will of life on his bed by studying with English dictionaries and textbooks.

One day, he attended a crusade led by an American missionary, Ken Ties, on a Busan street and received grace. Afterwards, he helped him in interpretation, read lots of Christian books, and began to realize the truth of the gospel. But he did not have the assurance of faith that he decided to fast and pray earnestly. One night while he was fasting, he met Jesus who appeared to him like a bright light in his vision and experienced the baptism of the Holy Spirit.

The night Pastor Cho met Jesus, he was called as a preacher of the gospel. He came to Seoul to study theology in 1956 and entered 'Full Gospel Theology Seminary' at the top of the class. In the seminary, he met his ministry partner and the future mother-in-law, Pastor Choi Ja Sil.

Pastor Cho is one of the most revered evangelists in Korea. He was a Buddhist until he rejected his religion when he was near death from tuberculosis. He says that's when Jesus Christ appeared to him in the middle of the night and told him to preach the gospel. So he did. When the country was suffering in poverty and desperation after the Korean War, he preached the gospel of hope through prayer.

When he was faced with his physical limitations, he realized the meaning of Exodus 18:18 "The work is too heavy for you; you cannot handle it alone" whereby Moses appointed some officials over thousands, hundreds, fifties and tens and delegated the work to them. He also learned that the early church used to pray and fellowship together in their houses, and realized the importance of raising lay leaders, especially women, in the church. (Romans 16) This became the catalyst of changing the future of the church.

The following week, he told all the officials about cells and built a cell structure. He divided Seoul into 20 big districts and told them to have a worship service in their houses with the church members who lived nearby them. When the church educated and appointed women as cell leaders, it contributed tremendously to the growth of the church. Consequently, men in the church were greatly challenged by the growth of the women cells that they also started their cell meetings. (Today, this district cell meeting is expanded to youth and children cells and the number of adult cell leaders, both men and women, is approximately 13,660.)

Pastor Cho gives thanks to the Lord for his 47 years of ministry, and has been sincerely serving 750,000 church members. In the early 21st century, the church's goals for next 10 years are to build 500 prayer houses and 5,000 satellite churches in Korea, and to expand global mission through internet broadcasting, and to enlarge overseas mission to the third world countries, including North Korea. For these goals,

The Present Pastor

REVEREND YOUNG HOON LEE stated, "Our church operates

like orchestra. Every day we make perfect harmony and fantastic symphony. People don't come to our church because I'm a holy person, I'm not a spectacular Christian. No! They come because I supply their need. I meet their need through the word of God.

His credentials reveal the ability to follow in the footsteps of this churches founder.

They follow:

-Yonsei University Th.B
- Hansei University BA
- United Graduate School of Theology
  Yonsei University Th.M
- Westminster University Theology Seminary Th.M
- Temple University M.A and Ph.D
- Professor of Hansei University and Head of Planning and Research Department
- Lecturer of Full Gospel Theological Seminary
- Theology Committee of National Council of Churches in Korea (NCCK)
- Chancellor of Bethesda University
- Dean of Japan Full Gospel Theology Seminary
- Committee of Asia Pacific Theological Association
- CEO of Institute of Church Growth Research
- Former Senior Pastor of Washington Full Gospel Church, Tokyo Full Gospel Church and Los Angeles Full Gospel Church
- Co-president of the Christian Council of Korea
- Chairman of National Council of Churches in Korea (NCCK)
- Senior Pastor of Yoido Full Gospel Church (Present)

- Chairman of Assemblies of God of Korea (Present)
- Co-President of Korean Diakonia
- CEO of Good People Corp.
- CEO of Full Gospel World Mission Inc.
- Chairman of Committee for Homeless in the National Council of Churches in Korea (NCCK)

New Creation Church

Singapore

30,000

Pastor Joseph Prince

Joseph Prince is a founding member of New Creation Church, and serves as the church's senior pastor on a voluntary basis.

Joseph Prince, the son of a Sikh priest of Indian origin and a Chinese mother, spent his primary school years in Perak, Malaysia.

Prince changed his birth name to Joseph Prince during his previous occupation as an IT consultant.

Prince has been invited to preach at churches in Australia, Canada, Great Britain, Italy, Indonesia, the Netherlands, Norway, South Africa and the United States. Notably, he was invited to preach at the Grace & Favor Seminar at Hillsong Church Sydney, and Hillsong London in 2006. In 2007 and 2008, he was invited to speak at the Hillsong Conferences in Sydney and London. In 2009, he was invited to speak, alongside Joel Osteen from Lakewood Church, at the 2 Days of Hope Conference held in Johannesburg, South Africa. He also preached two sessions at the 2015 Hillsong Europe conference in London during July 2015.

Prince's TV program Destined to Reign is broadcast in more than 150 countries. His broadcast program is also streamed online through Internet and podcasts.

Prince publishes books, CDs and DVDs. In 2007, his book *Destined to Reign: The Secret to Effortless Success, Wholeness and Victorious Living*, which contains teachings from his ten years of preaching from 1997 to 2007, was published in Singapore and the US. Six months after the book's US release, it was listed as one of Christian Retailing's Top 100 Books. In 2010, Prince's latest book Unmerited Favor, was published worldwide by Charisma House.

Prince was featured in the cover story of the June 2010 issue of Charisma magazine, which covered his preaching and teaching ministry.

On 29 October 2011, Prince ministered in the US for the first time at Lakewood Church, America's largest church, in Houston, Texas. He also preached at two more services the day after.

In his 1st United States Tour, The Power of Right Believing, he spoke in 4 cities all across the US. It started in the Prudential Center in Newark, NJ on Friday, 1 November 2013. Next was the Long Beach Arena in Long Beach, CA on Wednesday, 6 November 2013. Then he preached the weekend services of Lakewood Church, America's largest church, in Houston, TX on Saturday, 9 November 2013 and Sunday, 10 November 2013. The last stop on this tour was the Verizon Theatre in Grand Prairie, TX on Wednesday, 13 November 2013.

Passionate about God's Word and His people, he is a dynamic, humorous and anointed speaker who travels to minister to pastors worldwide. He is also a remarkable leader whose desire is to see people empowered by God's grace to live victorious lives.

With more than two decades of full-time ministry behind him, Pastor Joseph Prince is today a leading voice in proclaiming the gospel of grace around the world through his books, teaching resources, and television ministry.

The author of best sellers such as *The Power of Right Believing, Destined To Reign, and Unmerited Favor*, Pastor

Prince is also a highly sought-after conference speaker. He has impacted church leaders worldwide by preaching the unadulterated gospel of Jesus with boldness. He is known for teaching God's Word in a fresh, practical, and revelatory way that always unveils Jesus. His humorous, dynamic and engaging style of preaching has also endeared him to a wide spectrum of viewers who tune in to his daily television program. His broadcast currently reaches millions of homes across North America, Europe, Africa, Australia, and Israel on both secular and Christian networks.

A founding member of New Creation Church, Pastor Prince initially served as an elder and associate pastor. However, his unanimous appointment as senior pastor in 1990 marked a turning point in the history of the church, which started experiencing phenomenal growth. Under Pastor Prince's leadership, the church congregation has grown by more than a hundredfold — from about 150 to more than 31,000. He currently serves as the senior pastor of the church on a voluntary basis.

Having built and established the leadership and congregation of New Creation Church on the sure foundation of Jesus Christ, Pastor Prince is now actively fulfilling, around the world, the mandate that God has given him to preach God's unmerited favor without compromise. He heads Joseph Prince Ministries, Inc., an international, non-profit organization that seeks to build, encourage and inspire people with the gospel of Jesus Christ through television broadcasting as well as new media technology. Pastor Prince's ministry as pastor, teacher, conference speaker and author continues to transform many lives, setting people free from the heavy yoke of the law, guilt and condemnation by pointing them to Jesus and His finished work at Calvary.

Pastor Prince believes the best in people and is committed to helping them discover how they can reign in life through the abundance of grace and the gift of righteousness. His desire is to help this generation of believers understand the new covenant of grace and realize how greatly blessed, highly favored and deeply loved they are by their heavenly Father.

At New Creation Church, we believe we are God's beloved. He demonstrated this by freely giving up heaven's best, His only Son Jesus, for you and me. When we catch a revelation of this truth, we are transformed by His grace from the inside out. That's the beauty of believing and living At New Creation Church, we believe we are God's beloved. He demonstrated this by freely giving up heaven's best, His only Son Jesus, for you and me. When we catch a revelation of this truth, we are transformed by His grace from the inside out. That's the beauty of believing and living in Daddy God's love and grace! No matter who you are or where you come from, there's always a place for you in our church family!

New Creation Church is an independent church, and a member of the National Council of Churches of Singapore.

Core Values

• Serve Out Of Rest

We can be productive and effective on the outside because we have God's peace and rest on the inside. Serving out of rest is not inactivity, but Spirit-directed activity.

• People Matter

We love and value every person because each of us matters to the Lord. In everything we do, we seek to glorify God and edify man.

• Excellence

We seek to excel in all that we do because we have the mind and Spirit of Christ.

• Cutting Edge

We endeavor to be innovative and always at the forefront of all that we do. We are geared to the times but still anchored to the Rock.

• Honor

We treat each other with respect and integrity. We honour and submit to our leaders as unto the Lord.

New Life Assembly of God

India
45,000

Rev. Chalmer Earl Stubbs pioneered the New Life Assembly of God Church in the year 1983. A man of great vision, Rev. Stubbs led the Church for over two decades. His guidance helped build the New Life Assembly of God Church from a small gathering of four people to about 6000 people. He was passionate in his commitment to lead people in knowing Jesus Christ as their Lord and Savior.

It was a great shock to us when he unexpectedly went to be with the Lord. He was working at our Administrative Office on the 14th of July 2008, when he suffered a sudden heart attack. He was rushed to the hospital immediately. The doctors tried their best for two hours to save him, but failed. It was the Lord's time for his home going. He slipped away from all of us to join his savior and our God, the Lord Jesus Christ and with all of the saints through the ages and with other family members that had preceded him. The flock he shepherded, New Life Assembly of God, and all his many friends will always miss him.

Leadership Team

Senior Pastor – Rev. Arlene Stubbs

Rev. Arlene Stubbs, along with her late husband Rev. C. Earl Stubbs founded the New Life Assembly of God Church in Hyderabad. She now serves as the Senior Pastor of this Church. For many years, she served as the Minister of Music and Director of Children's Ministry. Her special joy is to write and produce cantatas and dramas for Christmas and Easter. She has also played a vital role in developing and growing the Carecell ministry and building a strong Carecell leadership team. Her genuine concern and love for people enables her to reach out effortlessly to adults and children alike and meet the challenges of a growing Church.

Mrs. Stubbs has two wonderful daughters and sons-in-law and is proud of her three lovely grandchildren.

Senior Associate Pastor – Rev. Valson Varghese

Rev. Valson Varghese is the Senior Associate Pastor at the New Life Assemble of God Church. He has been on the Pastoral staff for the last 23 years. As the Senior Associate Pastor, he is actively involved in the preaching and teaching ministry of the Church. While his

current ministry includes the many facets of Pastoral duties his passion is still to reach and empower young people.

He currently serves as the National Youth Coordinator for God of India.

Associate Pastor – Rev. Younus Samuel

Rev. Younus Samuel is serving as the Associate Pastor Assembly of God Church. He has been the driving force for Youth Alive services from 60 to 600 young people, each week. His love for the Lord and his passion to reach out to the youth through creative media arts has made Youth Alive a great place to "hang out". His enthusiasm and energy pull in young people to try out the delightful way of walking and enjoying a New Life with Jesus Christ.

Motto
WIN the Lost,

BUILD the Believer, and

SEND into the Harvest.
We declare that Prayer is our Priority,

Evangelism is our Passion,

Discipleship is our Purpose.

New Life Assembly of God

It all began way back on the second Sunday of July, or more precisely on 10 July, of 1983 when Rev. and Mrs. Stubbs and their two daughters gathered to worship the Lord at their home in Sainikpuri, Secunderabad. The first three services were held at the Stubbs' home.

On 31st July 1983, as the Church family grew, the meetings were moved to the conference hall of Hotel Karan in Secunderabad, and the first meeting here had 14 people in attendance. The Church continued in Hotel Karan for four more years, and these were wonderful years of blessing and growth.

With an increasing need for space and amenities as the Church family grew, the meetings were moved to a large garage of Apex Motors on Rashtrapathi Road on 2nd August 1987. For the next three years, this seemed like the place to be as the Church continued to experience God's Presence and enjoy His goodness.

Then on 3rd June of 1990, once again the continually expanding family had outgrown the space available at Apex Motors, and moved to its present location at the Millennium Gardens, Secunderabad. And through our years of worshipping at Millennium Gardens, God has remained faithful to His Word, touching and transforming the lives of our members, and meeting all their needs.

The Lord has graciously led us for over 32 years, and the Church has grown from strength to strength in fellowship and in devotion. Now, the Church Family remain committed to connecting people to Jesus and watching the change and growth in people and the Church.

New Life Church

Mumbai, India

70,000

Susai Joseph, Founder, President and Leader New Life Movement International and New Life Churches

Passion for God Compassion for People

When God chooses to partner with man; He begins with a man.

1950 – Bombay

God, in his sovereignty, chose a young uneducated orphan boy from Mariapura a small village situated on the out skirts of Bangalore, in the South of India. Susai Joseph came to the city of Bombay in 1950 with nothing more than Rupees 1.50 and the clothes he wore. Having endured a hard life living on the streets of Bombay, he refused to accept poverty and educated himself. Dissatisfied with life and seeking answers to life's questions God met with him. This encounter would radically change his life and his destiny. He was ordained Pastor of the New Life Centre Church, in Mumbai, in 1969 - a self-supporting church. This church was started by missionaries from New Zealand.

1975 – New Life Fellowship Association - Bombay
Pastor Joseph founded the New Life Fellowship Association, with its new spiritual DNA. A self-supporting ministry. He registered 'The New Life Fellowship Association' as a separate legal entity in 1975 and became its

founding Chairman.*(It was commonly referred to as New Life Fellowship- NLF).* The movement went through difficult times in the early years until July 1980 when the Lord gave Pastor Joseph a vision for the city of Mumbai, the Nation of India and the nations of the world. From then on New Life Fellowship began to grow in Mumbai and beyond as the leadership was propelled by this vision.

2010 - New Life Movement International Launched

2010 was a 'turning point' in his life and ministry a challenging year of change and realignment. Subsequent to a leadership challenge, in May 2010, at New Life Fellowship Association the organization he founded in 1975 and successfully led for 35 years; as part of the 'new way forward' he was led to continue his God given vision. New Life Movement International (NLMI) was birthed - the new instrument for fulfilling this Vision. Leaders, Churches and Ministries that choose to remain under his leadership were realigned under NLMI. (The Churches are now known as New Life Church)

New Life Movement International (NLMI) was formed on 4th July 2010 and launched on the 1st of August 2010.

New Life Fellowship Association, commonly known as **New Life Fellowship** (NLF), is a group of neo-charismatic, Evangelical, Christian Churches primarily located in India.

New Life Fellowship began in the mid-sixties as a result of missionaries from the New Life Churches of New Zealand who came to India in 1964 out of a revival that took place in New Zealand.[5][6] They established New Life Centre in Pune and New Life Fellowship in Mumbai. **Dr. S. Joseph** joined the Church in Mumbai and was soon ordained Pastor and became the founding chairman of New Life Fellowship. In India, it has more than 100,000 adherents.

Calvary Temple

India
100,000

Satish Kumar started his Walk with God at the early age of 12, he started to learn to recognize Gods voice and know Gods will for his life and ministry. This has been the secret of his success and has laid a strong foundation for his ministry over the years.

In 1995 Bro. Satish Kumar heard God's voice in his heart. God said" I WILL GIVE YOU A VERY BIG CHURCH "This was even hard to imagine let alone think. He immediately shared this news with his close brothers and started praying for God's vision and plan and purpose to be fulfilled in his life.

Bro. Satish Kumar never wanted to be a famous preacher and never prayed to be one. He "NEVER WANTED TO BE A PASTOR BUT ALL THAT HE WANTED WAS TO BE WAS A MISSIONARY PREACHING THE GOOD NEWS TO THE UNREACHED PEOPLE". But in Gods sovereign will God decided to make Brother Satish Kumar a pastor to the largest church in INDIA.

It all began in 2005.....when God spoke to him to start Calvary Temple Church. Though Bro. Satish Kumar was not interested in starting a church or being a pastor yet He Obeyed Gods command and started CALVARY TEMPLE with 25 people on June 5th 2005 in Kukatpally, Hyderabad, India.

Small beginnings can never be small when God is in it.

God has equipped Bro. Satish Kumar to preach the word of God with His power and authority. He adopted his preaching method from Jesus Christ, that is.. Preaching the word with illustrations and parables. This greatly helped people to understand the word and apply it to their daily lives. His spirit filled sermons have attracted hundreds and thousands of people to Calvary temple. By the year ending 2006 the church had nearly 1000 members.

God was with Calvary temple and was helping build the temple with living souls and as a result of this by the end of 2007 the church reached 3,000 members and in 2008 – 8,000 members 2009-18,000 members, 2010-30,000, 2011-40,000 members 2012-50,000 and end of 2013 nearly 80,000 members, and at the end of June 2014 nearly 90,000 members and present 2015 More than 100,000 members worship God in this temple. Every month nearly 2000 people are added to the church and every year 15 to 20 thousands new members are added. Probably this is one fastest growing church in the world.

By God's Grace and by the diligence of Bro. Satish Kumar and His administration Calvary Temple was able to secure its own land. Calvary temple moved from a rented premises to 12 acres of its own land. As soon the land was bought worship services were started under tents for a few months.

Meanwhile Bro. Satish Kumar wanted to fast and pray in the land for forty days. 40 days prayers started on 11th June and continued for more than 6 months.

After praying for 40 days everyone wanted the prayers to extend to 40 more days and so 80 days prayers began. After 80 days this got extended to another 40 days. For 120 days, thousands of people gathered daily to pray in spite of the bad weather and torrential rains. Bro. Satish Kumar was led by the Lord to meditate on the book of Nehemiah during these 4 months of fasting prayers. Everyone enjoyed and soaked in the word of God and as Nehemiah prayed for 3 to 4 months before God asked him to build the wall of Jerusalem so Calvary temple also prayed for 120 days.

On October 9th at 6.30am God Spoke to Bro. Satish Kumar to lay the foundation stone for the church building. By this time the church had paid a lot of money for the land and to immediately construct a church would be a challenging step. But Bro. Satish Kumar heard from God and wanted to lay the foundation stone and asked God to enable him to build the church in 52 days as He did for Nehemiah. Nehemiah built the walls of Jerusalem in 52 days.

During the church service Brother Satish Kumar declared saying" We are going to build the church in 52 days with the help of Gods mighty hand. We are going to lay the foundation stone on 11 November and will finish construction by 31 December and enter into the new sanctuary by 1st Jan 2013".This was astonishing news and came as a surprise to all the members! Can a church as big as a stadium with a seating capacity of nearly 18,000 be built in 52 days. Grace and mercy on the 11th of November the foundation stone was laid by Brother Satish Kumar's beloved mother and his family amidst many of Gods servants and church believers.

Though many problems and challenges were encountered during construction yet God kept HIS promise and helped build the church in 52 days. All the church members entered into the new sanctuary on 1st Jan 2013 at 6.00pm and celebrated God's victory and saw the work of His hand. Glory be to God!

Today Calvary temple has Five services

Pyungkang Cheil Presbyterian Church

Korea
65,000

Rev. Abraham Park Yoon-sik, D.Min., D.D., is the founder and Senior Pastor of Pyungkang Cheil Presbyterian Church in Seoul, South Korea. His ministry spans over 50 years. He is the author of the History of Redemption Series of books. 6 out of 12 intended books have been published since October 2007 and the books have been translated into English, Chinese, Japanese, Bahasa Indonesia and Urdu. Rev. Park is well known for his sermons which can last more than 2 hours without any break. Rev. Park is known to pray daily for at least 2 hours and reads the Bible at least 3 hours each day, and he has done this without missing a day for the last 50 years of his ministry. He has read the Bible over 1800 times!

Biography

- *Born on May 17, 1928 in Sariwon, Hwang-he Province, Korea*
- *Graduated from the Presbyterian General Assembly Theological University (B.A. in Biblical Studies)*
- *Graduated from Kookmin University (B.A. in Business and Economy)*
- *Graduated from the Presbyterian General Assembly Theological Seminary (M.Div.)*

- *Honorary Doctor of Theology (Th.D.) from Faith Theological Seminary, USA*
- *Honorary Doctor of Ministry (D.Min.) from Lael College and Graduate School, USA*
- *Honorary Doctor of Philosophy (Ph.D.) from Henderson Christian University, Virginia, USA*
- *Honorary Doctor of Philosophy (Ph.D.) in Biblical Theology from Trinity Theological College & Seminary, Florida, USA (see Photo Gallery)*
- *Honorary Doctor of Theology (Th.D.) from Knox Seminary, Florida, USA (see Photo Gallery)*
- *Award from the Prime Minister of Korea, 1998*
- *Award from the President of Korea, 1999*
- *Former moderator of the General Assembly of the Presbyterian Church of Korea, Hap-dong Conservative*

Church

Located near Gimpo Airport, the Pyungkang Cheil Presbyterian Church is located in Oryu-dong, Guro-gu, and Seoul. It is one of the largest churches in South Korea. The Pyungkang Cheil Presbyterian Church in Seoul, South Korea, was founded by its Senior Pastor, Rev. Abraham Park Yoon-sik in 1964. He is famous as the author of the world renowned "History of Redemption Series". The church is founded on the Word of God and emphasizes on teaching the Word of God from the Bible. The Church is famous for the abundant Bible Study Classes available for youngsters to adults. "Pyungkang" means peace and "Cheil" means first; so the name of the church in English means "Peace First Presbyterian Church". The Church has more than 65,000-member

Victory

Philippines
110,000

Formerly known as **Victory Christian Fellowship** or **VCF** is a non-denominational Evangelical megachurch based in the Philippines and a founding member of the Every Nation Churches and Ministries, a worldwide movement of churches. 82,000 members meet weekly at its fifteen locations in Metro Manila alone. Victory is also one of the fastest growing churches in the Philippines, it has grown 25% each year for the last 12 years. Its main office is located at 32nd Street corner University Parkway, Fort Bonifacio, Taguig City. 110,000 (2015)

History

In 1984, under Maranatha Campus Ministries, Rice Broocks, Al Manamtam, Steve Murrell, his wife Deborah Murrell, and their team of sixty-five students went to Manila for one month of outreach and evangelism. This gave birth to Victory Metro Manila. The initial outreach led to a congregation of 150 primarily college students, with expansion to more sites in Manila and around the country. Filipino campus ministers and church planters then served as cross-cultural missionaries to more than a dozen nations in Asia, Europe, and Africa It is a member of Every Nation Churches and Ministries.

By 1986, the U-Belt congregation spread to Makati, then to Dagupan, Tuguegarao, Baguio, Los Baños, and other Philippine cities and abroad. Victory has sent Filipino campus ministers and church planters to serve as cross-cultural missionaries in Afghanistan, Australia, Bangladesh, Cambodia, China, Guam, India, Latvia, Malaysia, Russia, South Africa, the United Arab Emirates, and Vietnam. Besides these long-term missionaries, numerous short-term evangelism and medical teams have been sent to more than a dozen nations.

Maranatha Campus Ministries was then dissolved in 1989 following controversy over the group's methods, including allegations of cult-like tactic. This dissolution was supported by Rice Broocks, Steve Murrell, and Phil Bonasso who were former campus ministers of Maranatha. After this, Victory became an independent ministry.

In 1994, Broocks, Murrell, and Bonasso formed Morning Star International as an umbrella organization for their ministries. At its July 2004 conference, Morning Star announced that it was changing its name to Every Nation. Today, Victory is a member of the Philippine Missions Association, Philippine Missions Association Member Ministries and the Philippine Council of Evangelical Churches.

That original group of 150 students in Manila's U-Belt has grown to sixty thousand students, professionals, and families, who now worship in fifteen different venues around Metro Manila. Victory has also equipped and empowered over 3,500 small group discipleship leaders who meet weekly in coffee shops, homes, offices, and shopping malls all over the city for Bible study, prayer, and fellowship.

Steve Murrell is the founding pastor of Victory Metro Manila, and serves as the president of the Every Nation family of churches and ministries.

On July 26, 2009, Victory celebrated its 25th founding anniversary at the Smart Araneta Coliseum.

On July 2014, Victory celebrated their 30th founding anniversary.

Doctrine

As part of Every Nation Churches and Ministries, Victory embraces the Statement of Faith agreed in the National Association of Evangelicals. The church also believes and accepts the Nicene Creed and Chalcedonian Creed (better known as Creed of Chalcedon).

Victory is one church with fifteen locations in Metro Manila and has planted over sixty-five churches in various provinces in the Philippines. As of 2015, more than 82,000 people attend Victory worship services in Metro Manila alone.

Senior pastors

- Steve Murrell
- Manny Carlos
- Joey Bonifacio
- Ferdie Cabiling

Victory has sent Filipino campus ministers and church planters to serve as cross-cultural missionaries in Afghanistan, Australia, Bangladesh, Cambodia, China, Guam, India, Latvia, Malaysia, Russia, South Africa, the United Arab Emirates, and Vietnam. Besides these long-term missionaries, numerous short-term evangelism and medical teams have been sent to more than a dozen nations.

When they began, the Murrells had very little experience in ministry and no missions training. Steve says the only thing they knew how to do was to disciple people in small groups. Steve calls himself an "accidental missionary" because when he and Deborah set out for that mission trip in 1984, they never set out to build a large ministry. All they wanted to do was to honor God and make disciples. Before that, they did a campus ministry with students at Mississippi State. In the first years of this campus ministry, they made it up as they went along. The Murrells thought their time in the Philippines would be temporary so they always kept that in mind and always knew they would eventually turn the ministry over to the Filipinos in Manila. Steve also calls it the "leading/leaving model." This was an "accidental strategy." They trained people with what they knew, and as a result, these people they trained were empowered from the beginning.

Steve believes that every one of us is called to be a disciple and make disciples. He says many Christians know that they're supposed to be a disciple and to make disciples, but most of them don't know where to start. Discipleship isn't supposed to be complicated. It can be difficult, but it should not be complicated.

Jesus is our model. True discipleship is not helping church people become better church people. It is finding people who don't know Jesus, introducing them to Him, and helping them follow Him. In <u>Matthew 4:19</u>, Jesus calls His disciples who were fisherman. They weren't the most educated people during that time. Jesus' message was simple: follow Him, "fish" for people who don't know Him, and fellowship with others. Steve says one of the most common reasons people don't make disciples is because they don't feel ready for God to use them. There is always some reason for not making disciples but the Great Commission in Matthew 28 doesn't say anything about "being ready." In the Gospel of John, Jesus turns to Peter and tells him to feed His sheep even though Peter denied Him. This shows that Jesus is much more willing to use us than we "feel ready" to be used.

An important key to discipleship is not to stray from the basics of grace, faith and repentance. We must stay on the foundations of the Message. The repetition, consistency, and staying true to the Message are more important than finding more creative ways to make disciples.

.

Yan Fook Church

China
10,000

Evangelical Free of Church of China (EFCC) was established by the Reverend Hans J. von Qualen in 1888. It established its first church, Tin Chuen Church, in Hong Kong in 1937. In 1949, a large number of missionaries relocated themselves south to Hong Kong when there was a change in Chinese political scenery. At the same time, the EFCC Headquarters was also moved to Hong Kong to continue the implementation of its goal.

Dallas Seminary Alumni on Staff

Chi-Ho Chan (**MACE**, 2000) Pastor

Yin T. Cheng (**MABC**, 1997) Associate Pastor

Jeffrey Chiu (**THM**, 2010) Associate Pastor

Carole Wong Law (**MACE**, 1993) Minister

Kwok P. Luen (**THM**, 1990) Music Pastor

L. H. Mui (**THM**, 2011) Associate Pastor

Wing-Chi Patrick So (**STM**, 1985) Senior Pastor

According to the Holy Bible, EFCC sticks to these 7 basic doctrine.

- Believe in one true God, Creator of all things and Lord of the universe, eternally existing in three person, Father, Son and Holy Spirit.

- Believe that Jesus Christ is the Son of God, being true God and true man, having been conceived of the Holy Spirit and born of the Virgin Mary. He died on the cross for the atonement of man's iniquities, so that man may be delivered from the condemnation and power of sin. Further, He arose from dead, ascended into heaven, where at the right hand of the Father He now the Advocate and High Priest is interceding for the saints. He is also the Head of the Church, and will come visibly again from heaven to establish His kingdom and to judge the living and the dead.

- Believe that the Holy Spirit is the third person of the Trinity, who descended on the day of Pentecost to glorify Christ, convict sinners, grant new birth, and to indwell and empower the believers for victories and holy living, and to unite them into one body, the Church of Christ.

- Believe that man was created in the image of God but became spiritually dead because of disobedience to God. Since Adam our fore-father sinned, all have become sinners, living under the wrath of God. Only through sincere repentance and acceptance of Christ's redemption, cleansing by His blood and regeneration by the Holy Spirit can one enter the Kingdom of God.

- Believe in the Scriptures, both Old and New Testaments, to be the inspired Word of God, the living Word of life, wholly truthful and trustworthy, and the final authority for all Christian faith and life.

- Believe that all men will be resurrected, the believers to eternal life and heavenly blessings and the unbelievers to eternal death in hell.

- Believe that Satan is the Devil, the source of all evils. He is working in the hearts of disobedient men, and will one day receive eternal punishment.

EUROPE

There are 45 churches in Europe that have congregations that are considered mega-churches. These are represented in 16 countries with the United Kingdom having the most with 14 and Ukraine with five. The remaining churches are Hungary, Netherlands, France, North Ireland, Sweden, Germany, Russia, Switzerland, Portugal, Belgium, Romania, Norway, Spain and Armenia.

Faith Church

Budapest, Hungary
60,000

Sandor Nemeth

Sándor Németh was born on the 21st of November, 1950, in Gelse, during the Communist dictatorship, when Hungary was under occupation by the Soviet Red Army. Németh grew up in a Roman Catholic family. He graduated from High School in 1969, in Nagykanizsa.

In November 1969, Sándor Németh was arrested at the Yugoslav-Austrian border for attempting illegal immigration, and was imprisoned in Maribor for six days. This is where – for the first time in his life – he turned to God and made a solemn oath: if he is saved from criminal proceedings, he will enter into the service of God for the rest of his life. A few days after this prayer Németh was released from prison, and the Yugoslav authorities – following their amazing decision – did not inform their Hungarian counterparts of the criminal act.

Once he was released, the first thing Sándor Németh did was obtain a Bible, and ever since then, he is a regular reader of the Scriptures. He settled down in Budapest and until February, 1971, Németh worked at the Hungarian State Television and the library of the Museum of Natural Sciences. Between 1971 and February, 1973, he completed his compulsory military service. From 1973 to 1977 he was enrolled at the Roman Catholic Seminary, and also sat in as a guest student at the Old Testament and Jewish Literature classes of Rabbi Sándor Scheiber at the Jewish Theological Seminary.

While studying the Charismatic Movement of Christianity, he came to the realization that he is lacking a true conversion experience. This took place in April, 1976, in an ecumenical prayer group, the members of which were dominantly from a Calvinist background. Following his baptism in the Holy Spirit, he immediately started playing an active role in the activities and organizations of prayer groups and home churches, which were generally located at private homes and parishes. He became one of the founders of the Hungarian Catholic Charismatic Movement, and through his personal influence many Catholic theology students and intellectuals arrived at a personal relationship with God. One of them, Judit – who received her English and Russian teacher's diploma at Eötvös Lóránd University, Faculty of Humanities, and who was a practicing Catholic at the time – later became his wife and closest ministry partner. They got married in April, 1977.

In the following year, the authorities initiated an investigation against Judit – who was pregnant at the time – for the possession of illegal Christian literature and the "influencing" of young people. At this time, Judit decided on giving up her secondary school teaching job. In order to make a living, the young couple had to work as house cleaners and were also forced to take up temporary jobs. In this time, Judit also translated at different evangelical, independent Christian and Charismatic churches and – being a trained musician – she also became actively involved in the music ministry.

In June of 1978, following their water baptism as adults, Sándor and Judit parted ways with their former religious traditions and affiliations, and became Full-Gospel Evangelical Christians. A difficult, conflict-ridden time followed: Catholic acquaintances, friends and family members did not while studying the Charismatic Movement of Christianity, he came to the realization that he is lacking a true conversion experience. Understand their beliefs, but rather harshly criticized and rejected their new faith and the new way of life that they were trying to realize. In this way, the young couple lost their social contacts and friends, because they were now regarded to be "sectarians." In 1978, Sándor and Judit established contact with the internationally known and influential Bible teacher, Derek Prince. Up until his death in 2003, the couple maintained an intimate, disciple- teacher relationship with Dr. Prince. From this point on, they received Christian literature and study materials from Derek Prince Ministries (which was initially called Church Growth Ministries) and other American Christian organizations – through illegal channels, of course. Judit translated these writings into Hungarian.

Faith Church is a major Pentecostal church in Hungary. The community is one of Europe's largest Pentecostal-evangelical Christian churches, and the country's fourth most supported church (based on the 1% tax designation to churches). It kept its official church status after the Orbán government's 2011 reduction of the number of churches.

Faith Church accepts the results and spiritual, moral values of both early Christianity and the Reformation, as well as other revival movements serving the progress of the

Christian faith. Faith Church is a strong advocate of Christian Zionism, and well known for its commitment to support the State of Israel.

History

Faith Church was founded in 1979 by a group of seven Hungarian believers, led by Pastor Sándor Németh, who leads the church until today. The independent Pentecostal-Charismatic church could only conduct its worship services illegally during the years of the Communist regime. Its activities and leaders were monitored by the Communist secret service. By 1989, membership reached 2000 people. In 1989, the Hungarian State declared Faith Church a recognized denomination based on the 1895. XLIII. Act.

Today more than 60,000 believers regularly attend worship services. The weekly Sunday service of the Church is regularly broadcast on live television. Based on the 1% tax designation to churches, Faith Church is the fourth most supported church in Hungary. However, according to the last census in Hungary Faith Church was not among the four biggest churches.

Faith Church follows the biblical model of the self-supporting church. It does not receive any other financial support from the state, aside from the 1% tax designations for churches and the normatives available to schools.

There are about three hundred local church branches of *Faith Church* functioning all around the country and beyond the borders of Hungary. All neighboring countries, Germany and the U.S. have local Faith Churches as well. The majority of local churches hold worship services on privately owned property. The largest is Faith Hall located in Budapest, with a capacity of approximately ten thousand people. Local churches in Pécs, Debrecen, Nyíregyháza and Salgótarján are also housed in buildings that can accommodate more than a thousand people.

Faith Church maintains elementary schools in Budapest, Pécs, Nyíregyháza and Salgótarján and a kindergarten in Kecskemét. The state-accredited theological college, Saint Paul's Academy functions in Budapest.

The Faith and Morals Cultural Foundation performs social services, provides aid to families, cares for the elderly and also pursues teaching, training, information distribution and cultural services.

Good news

Moscow, Russia
3,500

Rick and Denise pioneered three churches, a Bible school, and a ministerial association that serves thousands of Russian-speaking pastors throughout the former USSR as well as parts of the Middle East. As Rick began training and mentoring leaders in the early days, Denise also developed a women's ministry that is actively involved in changing the lives of women and their families today. Specifically, they minister to the needs of orphans, women prisoners, the homeless, and drug-and-alcohol addicts.

Positioned in the heart of Russia's capital city is the Moscow Good News Church (MGNC) founded by Rick and Denise Renner. The thriving congregation reaches out to touch the lives of people from all walks of life through the various outreaches of the church. Through these programs and the anointed services at MGNC, thousands have been born again, taught the Word of God, and strengthened in their spiritual walk.

Paul Renner serves as one of the associate pastors alongside his parents. Philip Renner leads the ministry to the youth. Together with their staff and hundreds of volunteers, the Renners are making a difference in the lives of people from all walks of life in the city of Moscow and beyond. Their various outreaches include a focus on children, youth, home groups, singles, married couples, business professionals, women, men, Golden Agers (elderly), and internationals from countries all over the world. Ushering multitudes into the Kingdom of God, Rick and Denise and the Moscow Good News Church are truly "teaching all nations," as Jesus commanded (see Matthew 28:19). Believers in Jesus Christ continue to multiply and be strengthened in this region of the world as a result of the Renner's pastoral emphasis to seek and save the lost.

New Building

Moscow Good News Church

Exciting plans for the future are underway as a permanent facility for the Moscow Good News Church is in the process of becoming a reality. Once this building is fully renovated, it will be not only a home for the Moscow Good News Church, but also a lasting hub for the work of God's Kingdom throughout this part of the world. Such a wide variety of ministry events and outreaches will take place under its roof. So many people from all walks of life will be saved, healed, filled with the Spirit, and transformed by the power of God within its walls. So many powerful gifts and callings will be launched into the earth from this strategic platform. This church facility will be a gift for the generations to come — for the multitudes who will find Christ as their Savior, worship God, and be trained in His Word in this place.

The new building is an answer to the unswerving faith, prayers, and sacrificial giving of our dedicated partners and MGNC members. Watch this website for important updates, and follow our progress as we renovate our new church home.

In a land where the Russian Orthodox Church dominates, one evangelical charismatic church is creating spiritual waves.

"The Protestant movement is growing very strongly," said Rick Renner, senior pastor of Moscow Good News Church.

Renner and his wife Denise are at the forefront of the movement. In 1991, the couple moved their family to what is now the former Soviet Union with the goal of reaching Russians with the Gospel of Jesus Christ.

Nine years later, in September 2000, they started Moscow Good News Church in the Russian capital city.

"Moscow Church is approximately 3,500 people in regular attendance," Renner told CBN News.

That's big for Russia, where most Protestant churches attract less than a thousand people to each of their congregations.

Reaching the Upper Crust
While the goal is to reach a broad section of those living in the Moscow metropolis, the church puts a special emphasis on reaching the upper class.

"Specifically, a part of our vision is to reach a higher class of people," Renner said.

That's because "they need God, too, and there aren't many churches that they can actually feel comfortable in," he explained.

Most Russians belong to the Orthodox Church. Currently, there are an estimated 30,000 churches dotting the Russian landscape.

The church is gaining more prominence after decades of persecution under the Soviet system. Yet, this newfound role isn't necessarily translating into regular attendance or observance.

"Most people don't even know the tenets of the faith," Roman Lunkin of the Slavic Center for Law & Justice, explained. "They don't have a personal relationship with Jesus Christ. Nowadays, it is hip to be religious in Russia."

A Whole New Experience
But Renner said something different happens at Moscow Good News. Those from an Orthodox background find the evangelical church community a whole new experience.

"Some of them are shocked!" he exclaimed. "Some of them think, 'Wow, I've only seen this in movies!'"

Along with the preaching of the Gospel, worship and style of music played in church is a big draw, too.

"I say, 'Hey, come to church. We have music in church and it is fun," Renner said. "'Like what, Gospel music?' I said, 'Yeah, come see it!'"

In addition to the main service, Moscow Good News has an active children's ministry that puts on regular drama performances about the life of Christ.

They also have an entire church dedicated entirely to reaching the elderly.

House Divided
Despite the tremendous success of Moscow Good News Church, it faces a huge public perception problem.

In Russia, charismatic churches are often considered cults. Consequently, the government puts laws on the books to restrict religious freedom.

Because the Russian Orthodox Church views the evangelical churches as competitors, they often side with the government trying to limit evangelical church growth.

"The official position of the Russian Orthodox Church is that everything besides them is a cult," Renner told CBN News.

Hope in a New Generation
However, a new generation of young Russians are emerging with different views on the matter.

"I have evangelical Christians who are friends of mine," one young woman said. "I enjoy talking with them and appreciate things they share with me."

"I know the Orthodox Church doesn't have a good opinion of the Protestant churches, but that has to change," another young woman said.

It is that sentiment that Renner and members of Moscow Good News Church hope lead to more Russians embracing the message of Jesus Christ.

"Capitalism has come. Many people are successful. Many people have made money," Renner said.

"Many people have huge amounts of money, and they've found out for themselves that it is not the answer to all of their problems," Renner noted. "And so there's a new wave of interest in spiritual things."

Kensington Temple

London
7,000

Colin Dye – Leader of Kensington Temple - London City Church

Born in Kenya in 1953, Colin also lived for a time in Australia before coming to London at the age of 16 to train for a career in the arts. Two years later he accepted Jesus Christ and in 1975 he left a successful professional life to attend Bible College. After graduation, Colin served in Christian drug rehabilitation, seeing many young men delivered from drug and alcohol addiction by the power of Christ. In 1979, Colin married Amanda. They have one daughter, Elizabeth. In response to the Lord's call to preach and teach, Colin was accepted into the Kensington Temple ministry in 1979. In 1985, Colin was called to serve alongside Wynne Lewis, who had succeeded Eldin Corsie as Senior Minister of Kensington Temple.

Soon after that, Colin began to experience a new and powerful anointing on his life as the Lord released revelation gifts of prophecy, words of knowledge and healing. In various missions around the world, he began to see signs, wonders and miracles accompany his ministry

and rejoiced to see dramatic church growth. Also at this time, Colin founded the International Bible Institute of London which is one of the nation's premier centers of training for ministry. Colin's vision to equip and release workers for the end-time
harvest is being fulfilled as hundreds of students pass through the school's various programs.

Over the years Colin has been closely involved in serving KT's vision to set up satellite churches. He pastored KT's first officially recognized satellite church in Barnet in 1985 and planted a church in Northolt. Colin became Senior Minister of KT in 1991 and, as a dedicated servant of God with a passion for Christ, is being used by God to build on the successes of the past and take the church forward into the Cell Vision.

The present church building was founded as Horbury Chapel, and used by the Hornton Street Congregational church, Notting Hill, in 1849. The building was used from 1935 by the Bible-Pattern Church Fellowship (an Elim Pentecostal Church offshoot founded by George Jeffreys), and also known as the Church of the Foursquare Gospel (not to be confused with the International Church of the Foursquare Gospel), when it became known as Kensington Temple.

The use of the building reverted to the Elim Church in the early 1960s, and the church as it is known today was founded in 1965 by the Elim minister Rev. Eldin Corsie. Under his ministry in the late 1960s–1970s the congregation grew to 600, and then to several thousand under Rev. Wynne Lewis (later to become the Elim Church's General Superintendent) during the 1980s.

Since the 1980s, nicknamed by members of the church as 'KT', Kensington Temple has planted 150 churches across London. Today, It has around 50 churches in its Kensington Temple London City Church (KTLCC) network. Over the years, many churches KT has planted have opted to become independent churches or to have an official status as a self-standing Elim church.

In 2000, Kensington Temple began to transition into a cell church, and today it has hundreds of cell groups meeting weekly across London. The same year, KT moved its offices from Tabernacle, an ex-BBC warehouse in North Acton, to Monarch House in North Acton. In 2005 the church moved its offices to Summit House, Hanger Lane, London.

The church continues to hold services at the Notting Hill site. Around 5,000 people attend the services every week. Among its many ministries, the church has a bible school, a performing arts school, an A-level college, a nursery, a conference center, rooms to let, a publishing company (Dovewell Communications) and a cinema

Today, KT is an international congregation drawing over 110 nationalities together.

At Kensington Temple we believe that God has a destiny for every person – a great and wonderful purpose for you to fulfil in your life. It begins with getting to know God through His Son, our Lord Jesus Christ. Once your life is safely in His hands you can discover that purpose and begin to bring it to fulfilment through His strength and power.

The goal of this website is for you to have an insight into the life and ministry of Kensington Temple, London City Church. And, more than that, we want you to taste something of that life and ministry for yourself so that you can begin to minister to others. Serving God and other people is the greatest purpose that anyone can find for their life.

Thousands of people are discovering the joy of loving and serving God in a community of like-minded people. This happens not only in our celebration services in the Kensington Temple building on Sundays, but also in the week day cell meetings in homes, cafes, schools and places of work. KT Notting Hill Gate.

Kensington Temple, belongs to the Elim Pentecostal Church and is a large, vibrant and growing community of people from over 119 different nations meeting in homes all over London (cell groups) and in our main church building in Notting Hill Gate (celebration services). Over the years we have planted over 150 churches in London and have ministries who are serving God all over the world.

We are working, in partnership with believers from every denomination to see London and the World won for Christ. These are exciting days of Christian expansion as the world wide church is rapidly growing. Our belief is that we will also see expansion of the Christian Church in our day in Britain and Europe. There are many lively, fast growing churches in Europe and our prayer is that many more will join in the move of God that is touching our continent.

The conviction of Pentecostal Christians, as well as all those who follow the New Testament example, is that the Holy Spirit makes a difference to our lives. This is what enables our Christian faith to be practical, relevant and lively. We pray that the Holy Spirit will touch your life and refresh you in your knowledge and experience of Jesus Christ.

Living Stone church
Netherlands
2,500

APOSTLE EDGAR HOLDER
As a young man, Apostle Edgar Holder moved from Surinam to the Netherlands in the early seventies and with determination he began to study medicine at the University of Leiden.

After about one and a half years, a fellow student invited him for a Pentecostal church meeting. And although Apostle Edgar Holder had a religious background and had been a youth leader in Surinam for years, he discovered that he too, needed a personal relationship with the Lord Jesus Christ. The choice he made that day not only brought a change in his life, it also turned his life in a total new direction after a while.

The years following showed that the hand of God was unmistakably on his life. It became more and more evident that Apostle Edgar Holder was gifted to preach the Gospel powerfully and clearly.

Apostle Edgar Holder together with his wife, Pastor Irma Holder with whom he has five beautiful daughters, serve as pastors of *Living Stone Ministries* in Spijkenisse.

Apostle Edgar Holder & Pastor Irma Holder founded Living Stone Ministries in 1993. Ever since, the ministry has started growing and growing by God's grace. The vision is to equip people with the right knowledge that we are world changers and we have to walk in the supernatural like Jesus did: healing people, delivering people, setting people free and inspiring people to do the same.

Early 2013 we moved into our new church building. God is raising the standard in Europe and all over the world. We are very grateful and proud that we are able to reach and serve the world from this Evangelistic Centre. A long side the testimony of faith that this new building is carrying, we proclaim that with God nothing is impossible for those who believe. So we have dedicated this building to the Most High as a 'Safe Haven and Miracle Centre to the honor and glory of His name.

Living Stone Ministries is also involved in many missionary projects. For example in Indonesia, Surinam and South Africa we are supporting different kinds of projects. In Tanzania we support 'The City of Hope' founded by Dr. John Chacha of Teamwork Ministries. Besides reaching the world with the Gospel of Jesus Christ we find it a necessity and do like to contribute to open up new possibilities for other people.

More than ever before apostle Holder has the desire to preach God's Word in a very practical way to the nations. Miracles, signs and wonders are associated to his ministry at the ticking of the clock. So many times he is invited to come and deliver a powerful message at several meetings and conferences as well in Holland as abroad.

MIRACLE AND HEALING MEETING

Ephesians 1:19-20 (AMP) "And [so that you can know and understand] what is the immeasurable and unlimited and surpassing greatness of His power in and for us who believe, as demonstrated in the working of His mighty strength, which He exerted in Christ when He raised Him from the dead and seated Him at His [own] right hand in the heavenly [places]."

At *Living Stone Ministries*, we believe in the supernatural power of God and the manifestation of the Holy Spirit through the believer. Jesus clearly commissioned us to do what He has done. His purpose here on earth was to show that a life without sickness, shortcomings, poverty, etc. is at our disposal again. Furthermore, that by His coming the relationship between God and mankind could be restored. In our midst we see the powerful workings of God's healing and restoring power. People are healed miraculously of all kinds of sicknesses as well as of emotional pains. Circumstances that seemed to be hopeless change in a powerful way.

During these Power Meetings we want to encourage, inspire and help you to activate your faith. Come and expect a miracle from God!

Every first Friday of the month there is a Supernatural Healing Meeting at *Living Stone Ministries.*

Emanuel Baptist Church

Romania
2,400

Emanuel Baptist Church is a Baptist church located in Oradea, Romania. Completed in 1993, it is the largest Baptist church in Romania and the second-largest in Europe. Emmanuel Baptist Church, Oradea, Romania, is the largest Baptist church in Europe with seating for 3000 people, but if you want a seat you need to get there early, as between 5000 and 6000 people crowd into the building each Sunday.

Dr. Paul Negruț

President of Emanuel University of Oradea
Pastor of Emanuel Baptist Church, Oradea, Romania
Former president of the Romanian Baptist Union

Dr. Paul Negrut is the senior pastor of the largest evangelical church in Europe, Emmanuel Baptist Church, in Romania. Listen to him share about his life and ministry with our church.

Author of *Revelație, Scriptură, Comuniune, Cristos, Biserica și Lucrurile de pe Urmă, Suveranitatea lui Dumnezeu și Sensul Vieții sub Soare, Nu este Bine ca Omul să fie Singur,* and *Biserica, Statul și Autoritatea.*

Doru Hnatiuc
Pastor of Emanuel Baptist Church, Oradea
Professor   of   Homiletics   at Emanuel University
Contributor of articles to *Creștinul Azi* and *Mesaj*
Editor of numerous books

:

Embassy of the Blessed Kingdom of God For All Nations

Keiv, Ukraine
25,000

Pastor Sunday Adelaja is the Founder and Senior Pastor of The Embassy of the Blessed Kingdom of God for All Nations in Kyiv, Ukraine.

On February 6, 1994, seven people got together in one apartment in Kiev to worship the Lord and to know His Word. They didn't even have an idea that they were laying the foundation for one of the biggest churches in Europe.

He is a Nigerian-born leader with an apostolic gift for the twenty-first century. In his mid-thirties Pastor Sunday has already proven to be one of the world's most dynamic communicators and church planters and is regarded as the most successful pastor in Europe with over 25,000 members as well as daughter and satellite churches in over 35 countries worldwide.

The congregation includes members from all spheres of society, from former drug and alcohol addicted to politicians and millionaires. Its high percentage of white Europeans (98%) also indicates that boundaries of racial prejudice have been surpassed. In the same country where

Pastor Sunday has been called "chocolate rabbit" and several attempts have been made to deport him, thousands join hands and support his mission to see Ukraine and the whole world affected and saved by the gospel of the Kingdom. Pastor Sunday is recognized as an unusually gifted teacher of the Word of God, with an extraordinary operation in the gifts of the Spirit, especially the word of knowledge. He receives numerous speaking invitations to several countries in all continents of the world yearly, as well as invitations to meetings with heads of states and other politicians.

Pastor Sunday's influence in the areas of church growth, prayer and evangelism has been noted by Charisma Magazine, Ministries Today and many other Christian periodicals. The secular world media, such as the Wall Street Journal, Forbes, Washington Post, Reuters, Associated Press, CNN, BBC and German, Dutch and French national television have all widely reported on him. The Wall Street Journal called him "A Man with a Mission" set out to save Kyiv and the Ukrainian President Yushenko

acknowledged his strong involvement in the Orange revolution for democracy in Ukraine. Former Mayor of New York City Rudolph Giuliani stated: "Sunday, God bless you in your important mission. When I next come to Ukraine I would like to be at your church".

In August 2007 by invitation from the employees of the UN, Pastor Sunday Adelaja was invited as a speaker for three sessions. It was the first time in the history of the UN that a pastor speaks in the main hall of the UN. There were 500 organizations and missions from different parts of the world and leaders from 30 countries that participated in these sessions. From then on the Embassy of God started its preparation to enter the UN and become a member of this organization.

The church's radio and television ministry reaches approximately eight million people weekly in Ukraine and millions more through weekly TBN programs in Europe, Russia and Africa. He is also one of the main speakers at the Global Pastors Network, organized by the late Dr. Bill Bright.

The church's "Stephania Soup Kitchen" feeds 2,000 people daily and ministers through outreaches to hundreds of needy street and abandoned children.

God has used the "Love Rehabilitation Center to touch the lives of more than 3,000 drug and alcohol addicts, setting them free from the bonds of addiction.

Pastor Sunday's passion for Nation Transformation has driven him to maximally spread the word of God. He has written and published over 80 books of which some have been translated to English, German, Chinese, Arabic and

Dutch. Also, thousands of sermons have been recorded. He organizes annual pastors leadership seminars where over 1,000 ministers regularly attend, studying the topic 'Pastoring without Tears'. His passion is to ignite these ministers with fire and power to transform their cities and countries.

Every year Pastor Sunday organizes Pastors Seminars that take place in the church. He is also the main speaker there. During this time more than 1 000 servants learn how to be a pastor without tears and learn the keys of getting success. Also every year Pastor organizes a summer and winter fast which aiming to equip servants with fire and power to change their towns and countries.

Nowadays, the apostolic ministry of Pastor Sunday has gone far beyond the boundaries of Ukraine, making him a desirable speaker and a Pastor to pastors in many nations of the world. To date, he has visited over 30 countries.

International Christian Fellowship

Switzerland
2,800

ICF (International Christian Fellowship) is a evangelical association of churches from Neo-charismatic movement, founded in 1990 to Zurich in Switzerland, the association has more members churches spread across several cities in Switzerland, Germany, Austria, but also in several countries of the world, including; Prague in Czech Republic, Leiden in Netherlands, Tirana in Albania, Siem Reap in Cambodia, Tel Aviv in Israel. ICF has a Bible College affiliate, the ICF College.

The groups run off the basic principles of Christianity. Participants are encouraged to evangelize based on the Great Commission found in the New Testament of the Bible.

History

ICF was founded in 1990 by Heinz Strupler. In 1996, leadership was taken over by Leo Bigger and Matthias Bölsterli, who emphasized an aggressive policy of expansion. Around 2005, worship attendance at the Zurich "mother church" peaked above 2,000 participants, and has fallen to around 1,200 between 2005 and 2007. International Christian Fellowship (USA) founded by Rev. Gonzalez in Chicago, is not an international conglomerate. Identified as international in that the congregation is made up of various ethnic groups and nationalities (Hispanic, Asian, African American, Caucasian, etc.)

Small groups

Senior pastor Leo Bigger (b. 1968) with his wife Susanne introduced a hierarchical structure of groups, called "g|12", consisting of groups of 12 people of which every group leader was a group member in the superordinate group, terminating in the group led by Bigger. In 2004, official terminology was changed from "g|12" to "Small Group". The graphical representation was changed from presenting the bigger couple at the center of a circle instead of at the top of a pyramid, but the topological structure of the system remains unchanged. "g|12" is conceived as a pyramid scheme, urging each group member to strive to become the leader of a derivative group.

Small groups are set in place to promote group discussion on biblical principles. Members are encouraged to start new groups if their own group becomes too large to the point of fair discussion being jeopardized.

Leo Bigger Senior Pastor, ICF-Zurich Church, Zurich, Switzerland

When Leo Bigger, 41, talks about his church that's called ICF-Zurich (the International Christian Fellowship) in Zurich, Switzerland, he references the mission statement about being "a modern church, right on the heartbeat of time." "Heartbeat of time means understanding culture, trends and the mindset of the people you are reaching," he explains.

I started to lead ICF in 1996 after finishing a Bible School (IGW). ICF is a place for young people who do not go to church. We constantly ask ourselves how church needs to be to attract people today.

One church, but four locations.

All location pastors meet to pray and prepare message topics together. Some messages are live from our preachers' team and through live-broadcast. Location pastors preach once a month. A typical Sunday service has big lights, loud rock music, creative elements like video, theater, dance or video, a preaching and a response time at the end.

The make-up of the congregation by language, culture, nationalities, age groups. What is the attendance on a weekend?

It's mostly young people from all kinds of backgrounds going to different celebrations. Every weekend we have eight celebrations on different days and for different target groups like youth, young adults, Gen-x, German speaking, Swiss German speaking, Latin people, and English speaking internationals. The preachers preach in at least four services in three different languages to 2,800 people every weekend. That is, I think, very unique.

The first 10 years of growth

At first the church doubled three years in a row. The challenge now is to get new people for multiplication with the right DNA. Not to get people from other churches, but put fresh Christians into leadership roles. And that's not always easy as they were new believers.

The building is an old factory, mixed modern and old and easy to reach by public transportation. Location is a very important factor.

A typical view of Americans of Christianity in Europe is that the church hardly exists in Europe.

There are state churches in Switzerland, Catholic and Protestant. Free churches (revived churches) are seen as sects. Only 0.4 percent is attending a church regularly in Switzerland. Most countries with Catholic history have more, but the fact is Europe is dead spiritually.

A Vienna-based group called Observatory of Intolerance and Discrimination Against Christians in Europe recently released a report that voiced concern over the ability of Christians in Europe to publicly express their faith.

In Europe persecution toward Christians has started: Live and let live! Believe what you want, but keep it to yourself. Media writes bad things about Christians going to church. Muslims are scaring people.

In places of employment it is often said you can believe what you want, but don't talk about it at your job. We believe that it is important and challenge people to say what they believe when they are asked and be a living testimony for the people, as Jesus commissioned us to be. When you don't say anything the devil has reached the goal to keep you quiet.

The report warned that discriminatory laws were preventing the equal exercise of freedom in the areas of speech, conscience and religion, while the introduction of equality legislation was leading to "side-effect discrimination" against Christians. How much of a problem is this where you are, or in other parts of Europe where you are working?

Switzerland is a humanitarian country – people are good, but criminality and immorality is growing. It's good to tell people there is a life with value and morals. People in Europe haven't really seen modern, innovative churches. They are amazed when they come.

Each person stays on fire differently. Friends I can share with and have fun with. Play golf to clear mind. Time with my wife and kids. My main motto: Don't let a day go by without having had fun and joy in what God has given me. I do not endure church, but I enjoy it.

A good team and a strong vision. It is most important for me to passionately build churches in Europe. Europe does not need old fashioned answers, but true, honest answers. It is better not to give an answer than one which is not true.

Calvary Temple

India
100,000

Biggest church in India

Bro. Satish Kumar started his Walk with God at the early age of 12, he started to learn to recognize Gods voice and know Gods will for his life and ministry. This has been the secret of his success and has laid a strong foundation for his ministry over the years.

In 1995 Satish Kumar heard God's voice in his heart. God said" I WILL GIVE YOU A VERY BIG CHURCH "This was even hard to imagine let alone think. He immediately shared this news with his close brothers and started praying for God's vision and plan and purpose to be fulfilled in his life.

Bro. Satish Kumar never wanted to be a famous preacher and never prayed to be one. He "NEVER WANTED TO BE A PASTOR BUT ALL THAT HE WANTED WAS TO BE WAS A MISSIONARY PREACHING THE GOOD NEWS TO THE UNREACHED PEOPLE". But in Gods sovereign will God decided to make Brother Satish Kumar a pastor to the largest church in INDIA.

It all began in 2005.....when God spoke to him to start Calvary Temple Church. Though Bro. Satish Kumar was not interested in starting a church or being a pastor yet He Obeyed Gods command and started CALVARY TEMPLE with 25 people on June 5th 2005 in Kukatpally, Hyderabad, India.

Small beginnings can never be small when God is in it.

God has equipped Bro. Satish kumar to preach the word of God with His power and authority. He adopted his preaching method from Jesus Christ, that is .. Preaching the word with illustrations and parables. This greatly helped people to understand the word and apply it to their daily lives. His spirit filled sermons have attracted hundreds and thousands of people to Calvary temple. By the year ending 2006 the church had nearly 1000 members.

God was with Calvary temple and was helping build the temple with living souls and as a result of this by the end of 2007 the church reached 3,000 members and in 2008 – 8,000 members 2009- 18,000 members, 2010- 30,000, 2011- 40,000 members 2012- 50,000 and end of 2013 nearly 80,000 members, and at the end of June 2014 nearly 90,000 members and present 2015 more than 100,000 members worship God in this temple. Every month nearly 2000 people are added to the church and every year 15 to 20 thousands new members are added. Probably this is one fastest growing church in the world. All Glory to God.

By God Grace and by the diligence of bro. Satish Kumar and His administration Calvary Temple was able to secure its own land. Calvary temple moved from a rented premises to 12 acres of its own land. As soon the land was bought worship services were started under tents for a few months.

Meanwhile Bro. Satish Kumar wanted to fast and pray in the land for forty days. 40 days prayers started on 11th June and continued for more than 6 months.

After praying for 40 days everyone wanted the prayers to extend to 40 more days and so 80 days prayers began. After 80 days this got extended to another 40 days. For 120 days, thousands of people gathered daily to pray in spite of the bad weather and torrential rains. Bro. Satish Kumar was led by the Lord to meditate on the book of Nehemiah during these 4 months of fasting prayers. Everyone enjoyed and soaked in the word of God and as Nehemiah prayed for 3 to

4 months before God asked him to build the wall of Jerusalem so Calvary temple also prayed for 120 days.

On October 9th at 6.30am God Spoke to Bro. Satish Kumar to lay the foundation stone for the church building. By this time the church had paid a lot of money for the land and to immediately construct a church would be a challenging step. But Bro. Satish Kumar heard from God and wanted to lay the foundation stone and asked God to enable him to build the church in 52 days as He did for Nehemiah. Nehemiah built the walls of Jerusalem in 52 days.

By God's Grace and mercy on the 11th of November the foundation stone was laid by Brother Satish Kumar beloved mother and his family amidst many of Gods servants and church believers.

Though many problems and challenges were encountered during construction yet God kept HIS promise and helped build the church in 52 days. All the church members entered into the new sanctuary on 1st Jan 2013 at 6.00pm and celebrated God's victory and saw the work of His hand. Glory be to God!

Today Calvary Temple has five services

New Testament Churches - Russia
**(Russian Church of Evangelical Christians
Of New Testament Faith)**

One of the largest Russian Protestant denominations is the New Testament Churches. Under the dynamic leadership of Senior Bishop Edward Grabavenko, this ministry launched an initiative in 2010 aimed at starting 10,000 new church congregations in Russia by 2020. Huge Russia stretches over eleven time zones and presently has more than 130,000 cities, towns, and villages with no church. Russian believers volunteer a year or more of their lives, at no salary, to serve on church-planting evangelistic teams. Every year, more believers catch the vision and volunteer.

As of 2012, more than 1000 new congregations had been started, and the denomination's Bible School has provided leadership for them. Because the missionaries serve without pay, only receiving food and lodging, the cost is a minimal $40 per month per missionary. A missionary who is called and sent to people who have never before heard the Good News.

The Perm "New Testament" Church in the RC CEF, which launched active missionary efforts in 1992, now has work in some 400 churches and fellowships in the Perm Region, in

The Perm New Testament Church – 3,500

Bashkiria, and in Tatarstan. Other notable regional groupings in the RC CEF include the Association of Churches of the Republic of Karelia (more than 50 churches and fellowships), the Pskov Church "Emmanuel" (some 20 churches), and the Murmansk Regional Association of Churches (more than 30 churches and fellowships).

The Pentecostal and Charismatic movement is the third largest religious movement in Russia, after the Russian Orthodox Church (ROC) and Islam, and it is growing rapidly. Russia is home to three large Pentecostal denominations. The largest is the Russian Church of Christians of the Evangelical Faith (RCCEF), sometimes referred to as the Russian Church of Evangelical Christians, with approximately 300,000 members, if children are counted, and some 1,300 congregations. It is headed by Eduard Grabovenko (www.hve.ru). It is followed by the Russian Association of Christians of the Evangelical Faith (RACEFP), led by Sergei Ryakhovsky (cef.ru). The third largest Pentecostal church is the unregistered United Church of Christians of the Evangelical Faith (UCCEF) led by Ivan Fedotov.

Differences among these three denominations today are rather small. All three are Trinitarian, all practice believers' baptism, all believe in healing in response to prayer, and all value speaking in tongues. Grabovenko's RCCEF has its roots in traditional Russian Pentecostalism and has had close ties to the Assemblies of God, but it also includes more Charismatic congregations. Ryakhovsky's RACEFP is an umbrella organization including groups of churches associated with various Neo-charismatic missions, including the Churches of Faith, but it also includes more traditional congregations.

The population of Russia is approximately 142 million, but is decreasing by about 1 million people annually.

There are 158,000 cities, towns, and villages and 29,000 of them are now abandoned.

There are 25,000 congregation of Christian denominations in all the country of Russia and 75% of these are Orthodox and only about 2% are evangelical Protestant Christians.

According to the Joshua project Russia is home to about 163 different ethnic groups and 77 of these are considered unreached are least reached. This constitutes 9.1% of the total population.

Pentecostals and Charismatics in the Russian Federation today is approximately 900,000 believers in four to five thousand churches and satellite group fellowships.

The Metropolitan Tabernacle

Belfast, Ireland

4,000

Opened in February 1994, our present building it is correctly called - The Metropolitan Tabernacle, Belfast. Just as London under that Precious Servant of God, Charles Haddon Spurgeon, had the Metropolitan Tabernacle, so we trust this province of Northern Ireland will have its own Metropolitan Tabernacle. The purpose of the building of such a magnificent sanctuary as the Tabernacle at Whitewell, is none other than to preach the glorious gospel of the Lord Jesus Christ and the edification and preparation of God's people for the greatest event in history - namely the visible, physical, literal second coming of the Lord Jesus Christ, back to this earth and the ushering in of his Kingdom.

The house is one for all classes, for all creeds, for all political persuasions. Our motto is found in the words of Paul to the Corinthians, when he says in: 1 Corinthians 2:v2.

For I determined not to know anything among you save Jesus Christ, and Him crucified."

THE CRADLE

" And this will be a sign to you: You will find a babe wrapped in swaddling clothes and lying in a manger".

It wasn't quite the stable of Bethlehem, but the humble beginnings of the Metropolitan Church Whitewell were no less obscure. That first morning on the 23rd February, 1957 it was snowing. The old Orange Hall which was rented, was still reeking with beer smells from the night before and a young man, together with a fellow worker brushed up the cigarette ends and opened the windows to let in some fresh air.

At just 19 years old James McConnell - an orphan boy from Spring Street, East Belfast was clearing the debris in time for his opening service. He had already served about 2 years as assistant to a Godly Minister in West Belfast and had also conducted some fine evangelistic campaigns in Ireland and England. Yet despite the offer of an attractive tour of Europe and the United States he realised that for him, the centre of God's will, was in the building of a church in North Belfast.

The first service began with just 10 People, plus 12 visitors making a grand total of 22 persons. One man recollecting the occasion, spoke with a smile as he recalled the young skinny preacher, announcing in revolutionary language about a great work that was going to start in Whitewell.

Indeed a prophecy followed which said - "You will remember this day. It is the beginning of months of tears, hardships and difficulties - but if you are faithful I will breathe upon you by my Spirit and give you a people that will touch this land. This church will become a reaping church and will benefit the community. I will bring into your midst hundreds of young people and many visitors will come to you by aeroplane and by ship to see what the Lord has accomplished among you". Thus saith the Lord. Here was confirmation that no matter what the circumstances or obstacles - God was anointing His servant for the task ahead.

THE FIRST TWELVE YEARS:

Except for the story of His coming to the temple in Jerusalem, very little is known about the first twelve years of the life of Jesus. The Gospel though tells us that, "He grew and became strong in spirit filled with wisdom and the grace of God was upon him". (Luke 2:40)

Equally Whitewell as a church was of no reputation in its embryonic form yet, unknown to our flock then, the leader was also a man blessed with a strong spirit and filled with an abundance of wisdom well beyond his years. Some-what inevitably perhaps, that same year James McConnell moved from his home in East Belfast to the Whitewell area, and thus began a romance which has lasted more than 39 years.

However, the initial grounding was by no means easy. In fact a lack of funds, and no congregation was hardly an ideal start to a pastorship - but as James McConnell would eventually prove, he was no ordinary Pastor and this was no ordinary calling. Day after day, from dawn to dusk, his main priority was to knock doors, and ask people to come and hear him preach. The main mode of travel was walking, as resources in the small church were so scarce he couldn't afford transport. Yet with God's help somehow, bills were always paid and people always attended.

Assisted ably by his wife Margaret whom he married in April 1959, the work quickly grew and like the great boy preacher of the eighteen hundreds, Charles Spurgeon, it wasn't long before people recognised his single - minded devotion to the cause of Christ and the conversion of sinners that resulted from his preaching. It was like a breath of fresh air for the people of Whitewell who marvelled at his youthful, but remarkably robust Pastor, who made no distinction between Protestant, Catholic, Jew or agnostic - as he saw them they were all precious souls in need of a Saviour.

EXPANSION

It soon became evident, that as a church, Whitewell would have to purchase a spiritual home of its own. Certainly if Roman Catholics were to be brought in under the sound of the Gospel this was imperative, as the by-laws of that original Orange Hall stated Roman Catholics were not allowed on the premises.

With ground purchased and plans passed, all our brethren, both young and old began working on that first sanctuary, but they soon ran into problems. It was late 1966 and the cost of designing a new retaining wall was estimated at over £2,500 - a small fortune in those days, especially for a total congregation which was still only in the region of 70. In fact when the project hit financial problems and major objections, that congregation was cut to 40 as roughly half made excuses and left.Just as Gideon was reduced from 10,000 men to 300, Pastor McConnell was praying that his depleted troops would rally round and defeat the Midianites of the modern era. Yet in those 40 faithful servants, God was already at work with the answers, as they laboured endlessly under the supervision of Brother John McAllister. The giving and sacrifice of those 40 warriors was outstanding. They were determined by the grace of God to build a house totally sanctified to His service. As for Pastor McConnell he continued to lead the line by extreme example. People knew he was a Pastor, who could preach but they were amazed then, as they are now at his willingness to go the extra mile. Each day for over 2 years he would be seen at that site digging, mixing cement, carrying bricks and negotiating with sub-contractors to get the best price. It was work that paid off as he and his loyal band of Godly men and women, not forgetting children, finally completed the project and moved into a beautiful new building (not far from the Orange Hall) on April 5th 1969.

What had seemed impossible had come to pass and remarkably with something to spare, as together they had raised above church expenses £30,000. Having spent the previous 12 years in a rented hall, that new facility was like a cathedral. Complete with a small balcony it seated nearly 450 people and was a marvellous expression of God's faithfulness to those who are faithful to him.

Throughout those cradle years, the Lord had taught Pastor James McConnell and his committed congregation what Christ Himself had said to the Ephesian Church in Revelation 2:2 'I know thy labour'. This labour was just beginning - as was the success of the Metropolitan Church Whitewell.

THE CROSS

The year 1969 signalled more than just the beginning of our first spiritual home. Sadly it marked the start of the troubles in Ulster, which have affected almost everyone living in the province - and the Whitewell witness has been no exception.

Those early years were fraught with danger as we were situated in the centre of a mixed community. There were times when you could cut the atmosphere with a knife. In fact on two occasions there were gun battles outside the church between terrorists and the army, leaving bullets imbedded in the ceiling of that sanctuary. The faith of many during this time was certainly tested as sectarian violence, bloodshed and bombing escalated to unprecedented levels. Various members living in flashpoint areas were frightened to come out as buses were being hi-jacked and set on fire. Indeed this was how the Whitewell bus ministry began, proving God adaptable to every situation.

With the province plummeting to an all-time low and the church powerless to bring an end to the sectarian slaughter, a wave of discontentment came over Pastor James McConnell, who had proved in every other facet of his faith to be a man of action. Something just had to be done and against the advice of certain members, James McConnell rejuvenated his old habit of walking, praying and knocking doors regardless of political or religious background. Indeed the next two and a half years saw a period of constant witnessing not to mention prayer meetings 6 days per week. At times it was frustrating as the work seemed void of reward however a change was coming that would shape the destiny of the church for the next 20 years. Pastor McConnell and his followers were about to take literally what Jesus commanded in Matthew 16:24 "If any man desires to come after me, let him deny himself and take up his cross and follow me".

DIVINELY LED

During the month of September 1973, while locked in the church on his own, Pastor McConnell suddenly became aware of a mighty presence. Initially afraid, his fear quickly disappeared as he recognised it as the same light that had visited him twice during his youth. Out of that mighty presence came the knowledge that souls were to be saved every week, and each time Whitewell would endeavour to do something with the Gospel, God in his grace, would confirm his word. This was followed by a prophecy which said "Have you love? Prepare to receive those from the dunghill: the off scouring of society. Love and receive them as I have you".

Almost immediately an influx of terrorists, alcoholics, prostitutes, divorcees, drug addicts, and homosexuals - both Catholic and Protestant, began to converge on Whitewell. People in distress, debt or desperation came and the Lord Jesus became a Captain over them.

THE CRITICS

Of course a move like this is not without its critics - even Jesus himself angered the scribes and the Pharisees. However, it was sad to note that most of the denunciations came from other denominations. Taunts were levelled against Whitewell as to the type of people that were being brought to the church. Yet the Whitewell people, who have always sought the inspiration of scripture were only doing what our Lord had taught the multitudes in Matthew 25:35-36

"For I was hungry and you gave me food; I was a stranger and you took me in; I was naked and you clothed me; I was sick and you visited me; I was in prison and you came to me"

Christ didn't form a glorified social club nor a fur coat brigade. He said in Matthew 28:19

"Go ye therefore, and make disciples of all nations, baptising them in the name of the Father and the Son and the Holy Ghost, teaching them to observe all things which I have commanded you".

Yet here was a new phase for Whitewell too - which itself was a little conventional Pentecostal church with neither the machinery nor the facilities to cope with the fish that were being caught in the net. It was a period of trial and error. Not all the conversions were lasting ones, indeed only about one in four grew to maturity. However, as it says in Mark 4:14-20 "The precious seed falls on four kinds of ground: the wayside, the stony, the thorny, and the good." One in four was not a bad return.

ANOTHER NEW HOUSE

The increasing numbers inevitably led to Whitwell's second major building project, which began in 1978. Once again, together with his colleagues and congregation Pastor McConnell was digging foundations and mixing cement. Sometimes he and his close friend Bertie Blake were so stuck in the mud and rain, they were left standing in their sock soles! The fellowship and comradeship never waned and in just 3 years by a miracle of God the new house was erected. Ironically the move came after 12 years - the same amount of time which was spent in he old Orange Hall.

During this time 2 more men came into full time service and the highly successful bus fleet was increased. Missionary endeavours soared too as Whitewell entered an exciting new era. Filling a church which had a capacity of 1,500 people wasn't easy as the current congregation then totalled 750 and the sight of an empty gallery didn't help matters. So the house closed for prayer repairs. A series of prayer meetings on Tuesdays, Wednesdays, Thursdays and also Fridays were implemented, as people were invited, willed or compelled to attend.

To the glory of our Lord Jesus Christ almost £300,000 of debt was settled in just 3 years and a significant increase in congregation was also noticed. Both Lord's Day morning and evening services began to be packed and many of those who attended Whitewell see it as a miracle that since the Angel of the Lord spoke back in 1973 not one unfruitful Sunday has passed without souls being saved.

Pastor James McConnell's reputation as a great preacher soon began to spread far and wide and by Christmas 1983 the church was being besieged by a deluge of journalists wanting to know why so many Roman Catholics and terrorists were getting saved and joining the church. Indeed four times over the next year the Whitewell ministry was featured on national television while also making the headlines in local and international newspapers.

Just like the Messiah, who was questioned vigorously by many religious authorities, Whitewell also underwent huge examination from established laymen and media alike. Yet, it has to be said that this publicity had no adverse effect on the Whitewell congregation. They remained a faithful, humble people and are, to this day, the same regardless of a greater swell in attendance.

God was truly working, demonstrated by the fact that no less than 66 people came to Christ after one particular Sunday night service. That marked the beginning of an awesome period of soul winning, where the Holy Spirit threw down all kinds of challenges to the people of Whitewell.

Lough. Like Elisha the Lord visited his faithful servant James McConnell telling him to build again. "Do not subdue the land - take it with all thy might" - saith the Lord

FOUNDER AND RETIRED SENIOR PASTOR JAMES MCCONNELL

From the founding of the Whitewell Metropolitan Tabernacle in 1957, at the age of 19, Pastor James McConnell served the Whitewell congregation as its Senior Pastor for over 57 years. During his years of faithful ministry at the Tabernacle, the congregation exploded from its initial membership of just 10 people, meeting in a rented Orange Hall, to the large congregation it is today. As an evangelist, Pastor McConnell also held gospel crusades around Northern Ireland, reaching thousands of souls for the Lord Jesus Christ. Although publically known as a hard-hitting preacher at the pulpit, Pastor McConnell also quietly helped many of our congregation through periods of sickness and personal problems. On 1 September 2014, aged 77, he retired as Senior Pastor of the Tabernacle, handing over the leadership to his then associate, Pastor David Purse.

Out of darkness God had brought light and unity ⁮
which for so long had known nothing but division,

"And that he might reconcile them both to God in ⁮
through the cross, thereby putting to death the
(Ephesians 2:16)

Despite adversity, God had built a church truly
"without spot or wrinkle, or any such thing" a ch
had felt the human sins of the world. One thing
earliest days had known nothing else but the Bible,
and the blessed Hope.

THE CROWN

As the scripture says "Prophecy is to be judged
comes to pass then it is of the Lord. That first prop
in the Old Orange Hall was itself about to be fulfi
most spectacular way. After all, months and
difficulties had been endured for the sake of the

Just like he promised, the Spirit had come ⁮
Whitewell the reaping church that was predicte
having now taken the Gospel to every town and
the province, Whitewell had become arguably ⁮
church in the United Kingdom. Remember the w⁮
bring into your midst hundreds of young people
visitors will come to you by aeroplane and ship t
the Lord has accomplished among you".

These words had been realised even before the
Whitewell's largest development so far, a se⁮
pound Tabernacle, directly beside the shores

SENIOR PASTOR DAVID PURSE

Pastor David Purse, the son of a policeman murdered by the IRA during the period of 'the troubles' in Northern Ireland, was ordained to the ministry in 1987. He grew up in the Whitewell Church where his father had been an elder, and Sunday School Superintendent. After entering the ministry, he first ministered in Newry, before moving to pastor two churches at Withernsea and East Hull in yorkshire. In 2008 he felt called back to Northern Ireland, and after two years in Cullybackey Elim Church he accepted the call to return to his home church at Whitewell, as the associate Pastor, and planned successor to Pastor James McConnell. Four years to the day of his return to the Whitewell congregation, on 1 September 2014, he succeeded Pastor James McConnell as the Church's Senior Pastor.

LATIN AMERICAN CHURCHES

Geographically in Latin America does not comprise as large of a landmass; therefore you find very few huge cities. However this region has at least eight countries that have 14 churches that will exceed more than 2000 with many a much larger. Guatemala has more than the others with four. Second is Mexico with three, with the remaining countries El Salvador, Honduras, Nicaragua, Costa Rica, Porta Rica and Bahamas having two or less churches considered mega-churches.

Harvest International ministry

San Pedro, Honduras
30,000

Located in an area of broad economic growth, with an area of 5 hectares. The auditorium has a capacity to accommodate 30,000 people and is located on the road to international airport Ramon Villeda Morales in San Pedro Sula. In Honduras, the complex of the Ministry international of the harvest, is one of the most complete, by the diversity of services provided to visitors to our Church.Pastor María Elena de Argeñal, was born in San Pedro Sula, daughter of pastors, mother of three children, David, Karen, and Alejandra, grandmother of four grandchildren. From an early age was highlighted by serving in different areas of the quadrangular, same Church, which was grazed by Evangelina Rosa Martínez and José Miguel Martínez parents. In 1977 she married Apostle Misael Argeñal, who thereafter undertook a commendable work in favor of the Kingdom of God. Pastor Argenal, is characterized by being a woman fearful of God, leading, visionary, sensitive to the need for the most needy, challenging and passionate to restore the life of each woman In 1996 in a time of prayer and fasting, God reveals him the vision that would develop through it to lift the lives of thousands of women who did not know and do not know what is his true identity as a human being and as daughters of God. Feel identified and charged with the need that many women suffer, it undertakes for the first time in Honduras the Mega conferences of women to impact Nations, events where annually recognized national and international exhibitors come together in order to expand this view in the life of each woman. During all these years a large number of them have been restored, inspired and challenged at this annual event where the glory, the love and the mercy of God is manifest. There are multiple ministerial activities carried out part of the Mega conferences of women, directs, and coordinates monthly meetings the last Monday of each month, where ladies from across the city of San Pedro Sula and surrounding areas attend promptly the auditorium in this Ministry for education based on the word of God. The regional congresses, performed with support of pastors of the various subsidiaries churches located in Honduran territory. His love and passion is not only focused on women, but also to children, given that in this country there is a high rate of orphan hood and in support Government with her husband founded the orphanage House Home light, Center where are housed infants who, from birth, were discarded by their parents and society. In light house home, are given love, atmosphere, food, clothes, footwear, strong Tower school education, medical attention, they are staffed by full-time. All of them receive spiritual training. Aiming to activate, train, teach and raise an army of intercessors, founds the school of warriors of the harvest. Classes are offered every Friday in the afternoon. Education is provided at four levels by highly qualified personnel. He is Director and presenter of television and radio programs.

Elim Central

El Salvador

115,000

Mision Cristiana Elim Internacional is a Pentecostal world ministry that was founded in El Salvador by Pastor Sergio Solorzano. It has churches throughout North and South America as well as Belgium and Australia.

Its mother church, a megachurch known as "Elim Central", is located in San Salvador. Once known as the second largest single church in the world, the ministry has a membership that surpasses 115,000 people and has, at its peak, numbered as much as 200,000. MCEI has more than 500 full-time pastors in El Salvador alone. The church is known for its *"Time of Restoration"* events in which hundreds of thousands of people gather from all around the world to worship together. These events have sometimes been held simultaneously in all the major sports stadiums in El Salvador. Its membership was surpassed only by the Yoido Full Gospel Church in Seoul, South Korea, a mega church with which MCEI has very warm relations. The church's senior pastor, David Yonggi Cho, developed a new organizational model (the "Cell Method") that would eventually be incorporated into Mision Cristiana Elim, which experienced dramatic success using it. As of today (2009) it is the fourth largest church. Javier Vasquez is

senior pastor of Yotabeche Methodist Church surpasses Elim Central with 150,000 members.

In May 1977, the Mision Cristiana Elim International church (which began as an offshoot of the Elim Church of Guatemala, itself an offshoot of Catholicism via Protestantism) began operations in a small space of the Santa Lucia de Ilopango in San Salvador, El Salvador with only nine people after an evangelistic campaign conducted on May 28 of that year was made official by Dr. Othoniel Rios Paredes, Pastor of Elim Christian Mission in Guatemala Bro Sergio Solorzano to lead the fledgling congregation.

Its growth

In 1983 the mission in El Salvador separated from that of Guatemala over disagreements as to their doctrinal positions, but the separation did not involve a name change due to the difficulty of starting this type of proceeding in the country which was still wracked by civil war. The church in El Salvador is still called "Misión Cristiana Elim de El Salvador" until today (the church in Guatemala changed its name to "Partners Area Elim Ministries" and later "Elim Ministries" (MI-EL) In 1985 the church in San Salvador had about 3,000 people, which was not entirely satisfactory. The church leadership decided to implement a .model similar to Cho's church pastor, Sergio Solorzano. The pastor of the mission decided to travel to South Korea to learn more about the work of Pastor Cho.

On July 13, 1986 the church opened a radio station named "Radio Restoration" which became one of the country's top after their kind ever since.

In the mid-1990s Pastor Solorzano experienced a spiritual crisis in his personal life that would eventually result in the naming of a new senior pastor to look after MCEI. He eventually overcame his doubts and went on to establish another world impact ministry, *"La Palabra Viva"* (The Living Word) in the late 1990s, which continues to flourish to this day. MCEI, now under the leadership of a new senior pastor, Mario Vega, also continues to flourish and expand.

MCEI owns 6 radio stations under the name "Radio Restauracion" in El Salvador and Los Angeles and is in the process of building an 11,000 seat auditorium and television studio in San Salvador.

Three different Elim's

In 2007, the Pastors Cesar Flores (Elim San Fernando Valley) and Nelson Martinez (Elim Guatemala) forged a division of enormous scope that separates nearly half of its branches within Elim Mission. They are still called Elim International despite winning the non-repudiation of dissidents and this forms the third Elim International with its headquarters in the capital of Guatemala.

These pastors divided mission Elim. Elim Internationally separating all of Mexico, Guatemala, South America and some of North America.

Amid the scandal over 33 subsidiaries were separated. Elim tries to recover the areas founding new churches and has established position denying any wrongdoing.

OTHER MEGA-CHURCHES IN CENTRAL AMERICA

"Friends of Israel" Bible Baptist Tabernacle -
Tabernaculo Biblico Bautista "Amigos de Israel" -
Pastor Brother Toby - Dr. Edgar Lopez Bertrand
(International Baptist Mission - Fundamentalist)
Colonia San Benito, San Salvador, El Salvador
Auditorium seats 10,000 people; has six Sunday worship services
Total estimated Sunday attendance = **48,000**

International Harvest Ministry of Honduras -
Ministerio Internacional La Cosecha Honduras
(International Church of the Foursquare Gospel)
Pastor General Misael Argenal Rodriguez
Located in San Pedro Sula, Honduras
Auditorium seats **30,000** people; total attendance unknown.

Iglesia Elim Central de San Salvador -
Mision Cristiana Elim Internacional
(independent Pentecostal)
Pastor General Mario Vega
Calle al Matazano, Final Colonia Santa Lucia
San Salvador, El Salvador
Auditorium seats 5,000 people; has five Sunday worship services. Total estimated Sunday attendance = **22,000**

10,000-24,999

Iglesia Casa de Dios - House of God Church
(independent Pentecostal)
Pastor Carlos "Cash" Luna
Km. 17 on Main Highway to San Jose Pinula and El Salvador
Near Guatemala City, Guatemala
Auditorium seats 3,500 people; has five Sunday worship services
Total estimated Sunday attendance = **15,000**

Comunidad Apostolica Hosanna
Hosanna Apostolic Community
(affiliated with Assemblies of God)
Pastor Apostle Edwin Alvarez Hosanna Vision TV
Via Espana y Martin Sossa, La Cresta Calle 1era., Panama City, Panama
Auditorium seats 5,000 people; has three Sunday worship services
Total estimated Sunday attendance = **13,500**

Iglesia Fraternidad Cristiana - Christian Brotherhood Church (independent Pentecostal)
Pastor Jorge H. Lopez
Templo Mega-Frater, Km. 13.5 Calzada Roosevelt 8-25, Zona 3,
Colonia Cotio, Municipality of Mixco, Guatemala City, Guatemala
Auditorium seats 12,200 people; has one Sunday worship services.Total estimated Sunday attendance = **10,500**

Ministerios Ebenezer de Guatemala - Ebenezer Ministries of Guatemala
(independent Pentecostal)
Pastor Sergio Enriquez
Barrio San Pedrito, Zona 5, Guatemala City, Guatemala
Auditorium seats 2,500 people; has one Sunday worship services.Total estimated Sunday attendance = **10,500**

5,000-9,999

Iglesia de Jesucristo La Familia de Dios - Family of God Church of Jesus Christ
(independent Pentecostal)
Pastor Luis Fernando Solares
Municipality of Mixco, Guatemala City, Guatemala
Auditorium seats 5,000 people; has two Sunday worship services. Total estimated Sunday attendance = **9,000**

Ministerios Apostolar Centro Cristiano - Christian Center Apostolic Ministries
(independent Pentecostal)
Pastor Augusto Marenco
Rotonda de la Residencial Bello Horizonte, Managua, Nicaragua
Auditorium seats 1,500 people; has six Sunday worship services. Total estimated Sunday attendance = **9,000**

Ministerio Internacional Rios de Agua Viva - Rivers of Living Water International Ministry
(independent Pentecostal)
Pastor Omar Duarte
Sector de Rubenia de Managua, Nicaragua
Auditorium seats about 3,000 people; has three Sunday worship services. Total Estimated Sunday attendance = **8,500**

Comunidad de Renovacion Familiar Hosanna - Hosanna Community of Family Renewal
(affiliated with the Assemblies of God)
Pastor David Spencer
Pista Jean Paul Genie, Managua, Nicaragua
Auditorium seats 2,500 people; has three Sunday worship services. Total estimated Sunday attendance **= 7,000**

Iglesia de Cristo Elim Central - Elim Central Church of Christ
Pastor General Hector Nufio
(independent Pentecostal)
3a Avenida 11-42, Colonia El Rosario, Zona 3
Municipality of Mixco, Guatemala City, Guatemala
Auditorium seats 3,200 people; has two Sunday worship services. Total estimated Sunday attendance = **6,000**

"Oasis of Hope" Assembly of God - Iglesia Asambleas de Dios "Oasis de Esperanza"
Pastor Apostol Raul Vargas
Moravia, San Jose, Costa Rica

Auditorium seats 2,500 people; has three Sunday worship services. Total estimated Sunday attendance = **5,250**

Misi�n Cristiana Mundial La Rosa de Sar�n - Rose of Sharon Worldwide Christian Mission
(independent Pentecostal)
Pastor Jose Luis Madrigal
San Francisco de Goicoechea, San Jose, Costa Rica
Auditorium seats 3,000 people; has three Sunday worship services. Total estimated Sunday attendance = **5,000**

"Passion for Souls" International Apostolic Community - Comunidad Apostolica Internacional "Pasion por las Almas"
(independent Pentecostal)
Pastor Apostol William Magana
Avenida 10, Hospital District, San Jose
Auditorium seats 2,000 people; has three Sunday worship services. Total estimated Sunday attendance = **5,000**

2,000-4,999

Iglesia Lluvias de Gracia - Showers of Blessing Church (Mision Cristiana Evangelica Lluvias de Gracia)
(independent Pentecostal)
Pastor Apostol Edmundo Madrid Morales
10 Avenida 16-70, Sector 5, Planes de Minerva
Zona 11, Municipality of Mixco, Guatemala City, Guatemala
Auditorium seats 5,000 people; has three Sunday worship services. Total estimated Sunday attendance = **4,700**

Iglesia El Shaddai - El Shaddai Church
(independent Pentecostal)
Pastora Cecilia de Caballeros
4 Calle 23-03, Zona 14, Guatemala City, Guatemala
Auditorium seats 5,000 people; has three Sunday worship
services. Total estimated Sunday attendance = **4,700**

**Centro Evangelistico de las Asambleas de Dios -
Evangelistic Center of the Assemblies of God**
Pastor Olvidio Valladares
Colonia Javier Cuadras Montoya, Managua, Nicaragua
Auditorium seats 1,000 people; has six Sunday worship
services. Total estimated Sunday attendance = **4,500**

**Abundant Life Christian Community-
Comunidad Cristiana "Vida Abundante"
(Federacion de Iglesias Vida Abundante - FIVA)**
(independent Charismatic)
Pastor Ricardo Salazar
San Antonio de Coronado, San Jose
Auditorium seats 2,100 people; has three Sunday worship
services. Total estimated Sunday attendance = **3,800**

**Eagles Nest Apostolic Mission - Mision Apostolica "Nido
de Aguilas" (MANA).(MANA Internacional / Kingdom
Takers Church -formerly known as the International
Charismatic Mission - MCI)**
Pastor Apostol Guido Luis Neez
La Uruca, San Jose, Costa Rica
Auditorium seats 1,800 people; has three Sunday worship
services. Total estimated Sunday attendance = **3,800**

Church of Jesus Christ "Palabra Mi-El" Central -
Iglesia de Jesucristo Palabra Mi-El Central
(independent Pentecostal: Mi-El = "Mision Elim")
Pastor ApOstol Gaspar Sapalu Alvarado
Boulevard El Naranjo 29-55, Zona 4
Municipality of Mixco, Guatemala City, Guatemala
Auditorium seats 3,500 people; has one Sunday worship
services. Total estimated Sunday attendance = **3,400**

Evangelistic Center of San Salvador -
Centro Evangelistico de San Salvador
(affiliated with the Assemblies of God)
Pastors Juan Angel and Edith Castro
2a Avenida Norte, Colonia La Rabida, San Salvador, El
Salvador
Auditorium seats 1,500 people; has three Sunday worship
services. Total estimated Sunday attendance = **3,000**

Joshua Christian Church - Iglesia Cristiana Joshua -
(affiliated with the Assemblies of God)
Pastor Lisandro Bojorquez
Avenida Mansferrer Sur, Colonia Campestre, San Salvador,
El Salvador
Auditorium seats 1,000 people; has three Sunday worship
services. Total estimated Sunday attendance = **3,000**

Family Worship Center Church -
Iglesia Centro Familiar de Adoracion
(affiliated with the Assemblies of God)
Pastor Francisco Karra
Colonia Santa Lucia, San Salvador, El Salvador

Auditorium seats 1,000 people; has three Sunday worship services. Total estimated Sunday attendance = **3,000**

Christian Temple - Templo Cristiano
(affiliated with the Assemblies of God)
Pastor Orlando Flores
Colonia San Benito, San Salvador, El Salvador
Auditorium seats 1,800 people; has three Sunday worship services. Total estimated Sunday attendance = **3,000**

Iglesia Cristiana Vida Real - Royal Life Christian Church
(independent Pentecostal)
Pastor Rony Madrid
Centro de Convenciones Ilumina
19 Avenida 16-02, Zona 10, Guatemala City, Guatemala
Auditorium seats 1,100 people; has three Sunday worship services. Total estimated Sunday attendance = **3,000**

Assemblies of God Christian Center
Iglesia Asambleas de Dios "Centro Evangelistico"
Pastor Hugo Soles Gonzelez
Zapote, San Jose, Costa Rica
Auditorium seats 1,500 people; has two Sunday worship services. Total estimated Sunday attendance = **3,000**

City of God - Ciudad de Dios
(Affiliated with Brethren in Christ Church)
Pastor Dr. Alex Alvarado
Hatillo, San Jose
Auditorium seats 1,000 people; has three Sunday worship services. Total estimated Sunday attendance = **3,000**

Dr. Alton Loveless | 190

A Look at Some of the World's Largest Churches

Bible Temple of San Jose - Templo Bíblico de San Jos�
(AsociaciOn de Iglesias Bíblicas Costarricenses - AIBC)
Pastor Reynaldo Salazar
Downtown San Jose, 200 meters west of Parque Central,
Costa Rica
Auditorium seats 800 people; has three Sunday worship
services.Total estimated Sunday attendance = **2,400**

OCEANIA

The three countries of this region of the world have 20 megachurches. Australia has 15, New Zealand 4 and Fiji 1.

City Impact Church

New Zealand

4,000

It is a nondenominational church of faith with Pentecostal beliefs based in East Coast Bays, New Zealand.

Formerly known as Bays Christian Fellowship, it was founded in 1982 by current senior pastors Peter Mortlock and his wife Bev Mortlock. It has now grown to around 3000 extended members (as of mid-2008). The church also holds regular Community Impact days to assist with a variety of social organizations, as they seek to put biblical principles into practice.

The church also runs the television program *Impact For Life* on TV channel Prime every Sunday morning at 9 am and TV3 on Tuesday mornings at 5:30 am, as well as on *Shine TV*. Internationally, the *Impact for Life* program has been screened regularly on the Australian Christian Channel, United Christian Broadcast in UK, Power Vision in India, Cook Islands TV in Rarotonga, World Harvest Broadcasting network in Fiji and Daavo Christian Bible Channel in the Philippines.

Peter Lineham, a Christian academic at Massey University states "City Impact is fundamentalist in doctrine which shows in its views of women and homosexuality, and is closer to Destiny Church than any other church."

In addition to the Auckland branch, CIC also built a new 1,800 seat campus in Mt. Wellington in 2010 (where there are now plans to expand the 1,800, to about 2,500 (add 500 additional seating due to the rapid growth of the church community), which CIC now has two Auckland campuses. Mt Wellington campus hosts services at 10am and 6.30pm on Sundays. City Impact Church also has a network of churches in the South Island of New Zealand. These are located in Queenstown, Invercargill, Balclutha, as well as overseas churches, City Impact Church Canada, in Moncton, Bathurst and Fredericton, and one in Tonga (that was recently rebuilt and developed in 2010 by teams formed by the Church.

City Impact Church Canada is based in Moncton and has two other locations in New Brunswick, Canada. The church's senior pastor Donny Legere has confirmed, that further locations in Canada are planned, but hasn't given any information to any date. The main church in Moncton has an 300-seat auditorium with attached auditorium for the youth and Sunday school services, and also a private Christian school (Rhema Academy). CIC Canada also offers different ministries like, Bridgehouse Ministries and the Gateway project. Executive pastor is Dave Maclean, youth pastor is Pat Steeves and woman's ministry director and member of the pastoral leadership team is Dr. Tiffany Legere (TH.D).

In 2011, City Impact Church earned a revenue of $10,000,000 – roughly $6.9 million of that coming directly from tithes. Because the church is registered as a charity, all of its profits are tax-free.

City Impact Church School

CIC founded City Impact Church School in 2004, where subjects include History, Geography and Doctrine, Language, Mathematics, Science, Art, Music, Drama, PE, and Kingdom Building, and teaches Years 0 through to 13 (Primary, Intermediate and Secondary school).The school was temporarily closed in 2005 by the Ministry of Education because it was not a registered educational institution.

Crossway Baptist Church

Melbourne, Australia
5,000

Crossway Baptist Church is one of Australia's largest Baptist churches and is located in Melbourne's eastern suburbs. Regular attendance at Sunday services is over 3,900 people.

History

Crossway is regarded as a contemporary Baptist church, with Bible-based preaching.

The church was founded by the Reverend J.H Newnham in 1954. Subsequent senior pastors were the Reverend George Ashworth, the Reverend David Griffiths, the Reverend Rowland Croucher and the Reverend Stuart Robinson.

Previously known as Blackburn Baptist, the church is now on its third site. It originally met in a small hall as a Sunday school class on the corner of Holland and Canterbury Roads in Blackburn South. The church then relocated to 19 Holland Road, Blackburn South (now the headquarters of the Evangelical Chinese Church Melbourne), following large-scale growth.

The church then relocated to its current September 1995. Shortly after this relocation, the church changed its name to Crossway Baptist Church in order to reflect the congregation's regional nature. The church now enjoys a site of 15 acres (61,000 m^2) in the center of Melbourne's expansive eastern suburbs.

Robinson, a former missionary, founded the church at its current location and is now regarded as the founding pastor of Crossway. He has written three books including *Mosques and Miracles*, a book about Islam written from a Christian perspective and two books on prayer. Pastor Dale Stephenson, formerly from New Peninsula Baptist Church, replaced Stuart Robinson as senior pastor in February 2008. Stephenson leads a large team of approximately 65 staff and many hundreds of volunteers.

Present

Crossway has a large number of ministries for all ages, including a children's ministry called "Kidspace", a youth ministry called "Surge", a young adults ministry called "Vive" and ministries for the elderly with a "50+" service. It also has a wide range of community services, with a significant "Care" network and a large community care ministry (called "LifeCare") offering professional counselling services, financial education and a supported mentoring program. Crossway also runs several midweek programs, including the Mothers of Preschoolers Program through MOPS International.

Crossway has planted daughter churches in Craigieburn, Cranbourne, Moreland and Stonnington as well as a number of other smaller experimental church plants.

Crossway also has language-based congregations with Mandarin, Cantonese, Indonesian and Korean services.

Since 2006, Crossway has also co-organized "Unite" - a creative arts conference featuring Australian musicians such as Roma Waterman and Michael Paynter. The conference is organized together with Gateway Church, Careforce Church and Christian City Church Whitehorse.

Crossway recently completed a building extension program, which was formally opened on 13 December 2009 by Senior Pastor Dale Stephenson. The extension includes a fully equipped cafe and dining area, larger meeting areas and a large elevator constructed to increase access for members. The coffee shop has become a thriving hub for the church and surrounding area, serving quality coffee and meals on weekdays and Sundays.

Crossway was one of the first churches in Australia to release a dedicated iPhone/Android app. The Crossway app offers direct access to audio and video sermons, church blogs and its calendar of events.

Copies of services on CD and or DVD can be purchased from Crossway after each Sunday service, and are also freely available online at Crossway's website and on iTunes.

Hillsong Church

Sydney Australia

31,400

It is a Pentecostal megachurch affiliated with Australian Christian Churches (the Australian branch of the Assemblies of God) and located in Sydney, New South Wales, Australia. The church was founded in 1983 when the Sydney Christian Life Centre at Waterloo, which was established by Frank Houston, merged with the Hills Christian Life Centre in Baulkham Hills, established by his son, Brian Houston.

While headquartered at its "Hills" location in Baulkham Hills' Norwest Business Park in the Hills District of Sydney, Hillsong is a multi-site church with campuses in Sydney, Brisbane, Melbourne, Newcastle, Gold Coast and Noosa. Its second campus, designated as the "City" campus, is located in Waterloo, near Sydney's central business district. In 2009, a third Sydney campus, "South West", located in Campbelltown and a fourth interstate location, the "Brisbane" campus in Mount Gravatt, Queensland were added. In 2012 it was announced that a fifth campus, also interstate, was to be opened in late 2012 or early 2013 in

Melbourne, Victoria. Additionally, Hillsong Church currently has 12 extension services across Sydney.

Hillsong Church's international offshoots include Hillsong Church London in the United Kingdom, Hillsong Church Kiev in Ukraine, Hillsong Church Cape Town and Hillsong Church Pretoria in South Africa, Hillsong Church Stockholm in Sweden and Hillsong NYC in New York, United States. Hillsong services are also held in Hillsong Church Paris in Paris, France, Hillsong Connect Group Lyon in Lyon, Hillsong Church Germany in Konstanz and Düsseldorf, Hillsong Church Amsterdam in Amsterdam, Hillsong Barcelona in Barcelona, Hillsong Church Copenhagen in Copenhagen, Hillsong Church Moscow in Moscow, Hillsong Church in Los Angeles and soon Hillsong Church Buenos Aires in Argentina and Hillsong Church São Paulo in Brazil.

Hillsong Music has topped Australian charts, with albums having achieved gold and platinum sales status. Hillsong is well-known through its teaching, album sales and annual Hillsong Conference. According to the church, over 30,000 people attend services each week.

Brian and Bobbie Houston moved from New Zealand in 1978 and joined the Sydney Christian Life Centre in Darlinghurst, pastored by Brian Houston's father, Frank Houston. They started Hillsong Church, which was then known as Hills Christian Life Centre, in August 1983 with services held at the Baulkham Hills Public School hall and with an initial congregation of 45. In 1990, the church moved from "the warehouse", which they had occupied since 1984, to hold services at the Hills Centre. In 1986, an annual conference was developed, now called Hillsong Conference.

Early Hills Christian Life Centre logo

In the early 1990s, praise and worship recordings from the Hills Christian Life Centre were released in Australia and internationally under the name Hillsong. The name is also used for a television show featuring clips from the videos of the recordings and a message from Brian Houston. In 1997 the church moved into its new building at Baulkham Hills' Norwest Business Park.

In the late 1990s the church realized that the name Hillsong was more well-known than Hills Christian Life Centre due to the branding of its recordings. The church was renamed Hillsong Church in 1999, about the same time its mother church, Sydney Christian Life Centre, was merged into Hillsong Church.

A new convention center at the church's "Hills" location, was opened on 19 October 2002 by John Howard, the then Prime Minister of Australia. Due to the growth of the "City" location, in 2007 the church announced its intentions to develop a significant area of land on Rothschild Avenue, Rosebery into the new "City" location. [In August 2008, Hillsong withdrew the development application they had lodged with the Sydney City Council after an independent report recommended against the council approving the development. Since then, Hillsong has opened up another City location in Alexandria.

Extensions

In the 1990s, Kiev Christian life Centre, now Hillsong Kiev, and London Christian Life Centre, now Hillsong London, were planted from the Hillsong Church as independent churches. When Hills Christian Life Centre changed its name to Hillsong Church the international churches also did so.

Hillsong London have planted extension services in Surrey and in Paris. In March 2007, Hillsong Kiev planted an offshoot church in Moscow, which started regular services in July 2007. It was announced in October 2007 that Phil and Lucinda Dooley would plant a Hillsong Church in South Africa in March 2008. Hillsong Stockholm, Sweden, formerly known as Passion Church, was planted in 2008-2009.[15] The senior pastor at Stockholm is Andreas Nielsen,

As Hillsong has grown, other churches have joined and new churches established as extension services. Extension services are also held for cultural groups in other languages. These extension services are run by a team of people but look to Hillsong Church for leadership and support and join the vision of the church. There are currently 15 extension services across Sydney, many of which join with the "Hills" and "City" congregations for Sunday night services. In September 2007, Brian Houston's son Ben planted the 15th extension service in Mona Vale, known as the Northern Beaches service. In August 2008, Hillsong started a Sunday morning service at the Greater Union Cinema at Bondi Junction, this service being part of the City location.

Beliefs

The church's beliefs are Evangelical and Pentecostal in that it holds the Bible as accurate and authoritative in matters of faith and that Jesus Christ is the Messiah, who reconciled humanity to God through his death and resurrection. The church believes that to live a fruitful Christian life a person should seek the baptism in the Holy Spirit and that the Holy Spirit enables the use of spiritual gifts, which includes, and is not limited to, speaking in tongues.

Hillsong's stand on many topical issues in contemporary Christianity is in keeping with mainstream Pentecostalism opposing embryonic stem cell research and abortion on the basis that human life commences at conception. Hillsong has also declared support for Creationism and Intelligent Design and believes this should be taught in schools. It also believes that homosexuality is contrary to biblical teaching but emphasizes that it does not condemn homosexuals.

Hillsong's prosperity teachings have been criticized by Christian leaders Tim Costello and George Pell. Subsequent statements by Tim Costello indicated that he was satisfied with changes made by Brian Houston to Hillsong's teaching in response to criticism, a change which has been noted by the media. Hillsong's teachings have been commented on favourably by Peter Costello, Tim Costello's brother, also a Baptist and a former Treasurer of Australia who has defended the church against accusations of unorthodoxy.

Leadership

The senior pastors of Hillsong Church are currently Brian and Bobbie Houston. They have been the pastors of the church since it was founded by Brian Houston in 1983.

Hillsong Church is also governed by a board of elders. The elders lead the church spiritually as well as act as a board of directors. The members of "The Hillsong Eldership" are senior executive staff and business leaders from Hillsong's congregation. Elders are appointed for one year renewable terms. Leadership positions are made by appointment.

Ministry

Hillsong Church runs many different ministries in addition to weekend services and events. Hillsong, like other churches, runs a small group structure named "connect groups". Groups of approximately 10-20 people meet on a fortnightly basis across Sydney. The main ministries of Hillsong Church include:

Life Church

Auckland, New Zealand

4,000

Founded as 'Auckland Christian Fellowship' (ACF) the church was birthed at a tent crusade run by Rob & Beryl Wheeler and a team from Tauranga on 10th November 1964.

After using several rented halls the church was able to purchase 'Haddon Hall' in central Auckland for their permanent home. The church has always had a vision to train new leaders. Over its lifetime it has supported the work of several bible colleges.

In 1979 Haddon Hall was sold to purchase the old Karitane Hospital in Mt Albert to house the newly formed Christian College 'Hebron'. At the same time Auckland Christian Fellowship began meeting at Epsom Girls Grammar School to allow the college full use of the Mt Albert site. Auckland Christian Fellowship released Hebron Christian College in 1990 to become an independent trust-run school.

In October 1991 Bruce and Maude McDonald became the Senior Ministers of Auckland Christian Fellowship, and in 2000 Bruce became the National Leader of the New Life Churches of New Zealand, and held that office for three years.

2002 saw 'Auckland Christian Fellowship' (ACF) become 'The Life Church'. We have a passion to enable people to find answers to all of life's challenges and have developed the primary vision of the church called 'Pathways'. The name 'The Life Church' was inspired by the scripture found in John 10:10 (NIV) where Jesus says: **"The thief comes only to steal and kill and destroy; I have come that they may have life, and have it to the full."** 2002 was a year of new beginnings for the church, as this new name was brings with it a new era for the church, with new opportunities and fresh vision. The church itself, though, is in fact over 40 years old, with a fascinating history and an undying passion to love and serve God.

In 2005 The Life Church in conjunction with Phlair International Colleges purchased the property at 60 Rockfield Road, Penrose. After a large reconstruction program the College and Church offices moved in, and with a continuing program of construction of the auditorium and cafe areas, providing a place to meet after church.

2014 saw some large changes at The Life Church, we celebrated our 50th birthday as a church, quite a milestone. Bruce and Maude McDonald also stepped down as the Senior Ministers of the church. After a short period new Pastors Peter and Cara Perumalla became the new Senior Pastors of The Life Church.

Planetshakers Church

Melbourne, Australia

10,000

Russell Evans is the Senior Pastor of Planetshakers Church, alongside his wife Sam and children, Jonathan and Aimee. As one of the leading international communicators of this generation, Russell's passion and hunger for encountering the Presence of God inspires all to exercise new levels of faith and take hold of the promises of God's Word.

Enjoying close relationships with many of the world's leading ministers, Russell is well known for his collaborative approach to building God's kingdom. He has the rare capacity to relate equally to both younger and older generations of people due to his rich heritage and experience along with a passion for fresh music and empowerment of emerging leaders. He has committed his life to "empower generations to win generations."

Planetshakers Church (formerly **Melbourne City Church**) is a Pentecostal Christian church affiliated with Australian Christian Churches, the Assemblies of God in Australia. The church started when the Planetshakers band and ministry moved to Melbourne in 2004. The church is pastored by Russell and Sam Evans and has over 10,000 members. Currently, Planetshakers has 4 campuses in Melbourne; City, North East, South East and Geelong, with an additional 2 international campuses; Cape Town, South Africa and Los

Angeles, USA. Its founder, Russell Evans, declared its aims "I believe that the church of God should be the greatest party on the planet... We're here not just to be local, we're here to be global and we can have the ability to influence the whole planet."

Riverview Church

Perth, Western Australia
4,500

It is a charismatic evangelical Christian church situated in Burswood, an inner suburb of Perth, Western Australia, and was originally established in 1979. The church is the largest in Western Australia with 4,500 members, led by Senior Minister Haydn Nelson.

History

The church was founded by the former pastor, Phil Baker's father, Brian J. Baker, who was born in England and with his wife, Valerie, migrated to New Zealand in 1972 and ran various ministries there. They subsequently trained at Rhema Bible Church in Tulsa, Oklahoma under Pastor Kenneth E. Hagin, and started the Inner City Faith Fellowship at Holmes Hall In Belmont, a suburb of Perth, on 9 December 1979. The church moved five months later to Brisbane Street, five blocks north of Perth's central business district. Baker was ordained by Hagin in 1980. At this time, the Bakers were assisted by Pastors Mark and Joanne Willhite and Pastors Mike and Randa Moorhead from Kansas City, who returned overseas after helping to establish Faith Christian Academy, which in February 1982 commenced teaching 70 school students from years 1 to 10 within the church's building.

The church changed name to Rhema Faith Fellowship in 1982 and again to Rhema Family Church in June 1985, also moving to its current premises at Burswood (then called Victoria Park), which previously operated as a warehouse. The school, renamed Rhema Christian Academy in 1985, had grown to 200 students by the following year and had moved to premises in Colombo Street, across Albany Highway from the church. A bible school (Rhema Bible Training Centre or RBTC) was opened, and in the spirit of its evangelical traditions, started churches around Western Australia and Australia, as well as over 100 home groups operating in Perth's suburbs. At its peak in the late 1980s, Rhema claimed to have over 3,200 members at its church in Victoria Park and was the biggest single church in Western Australia. By 1989, the church also offered a children's ministry during its main service for those up to the age of 15, divided into four age groups.

In April 1989, Brian Baker and his youngest son, Barnaby who was a Youth pastor in the church, travelled to the USA and both spoke at a number of churches, mostly in Texas and California. On their return, Brians wife Valerie who had been a pastor in the church and leader of the ladies ministry had decided to resign from the ministry. On 30 April 1989, Brian Baker announced that he would also resign from the ministry as their marriage had finally failed. Brian then appointed his older son Philip as the pastor and leader of the church. Philip was well known to the congregation as a teacher in many of the main services and Brian believed that the transition would save the church from disintegration after his and Valerie's resignations. Philip also a graduate of Rhema Bible Training Center in Tulsa had been working with his father in the church in recent years as the Dean of RBTC and previous pastor of the Children's ministry in the church. Philip and his wife Heather had been running a children's ministry in New Zealand prior to their return to Perth. Phil instituted a financial management plan for the church to handle mounting debts and liabilities arising from the late 1980s recession, including disbanding the nationwide Rhema branding for churches started by RBTC graduates and loosening the relationship with the school, now renamed Regent College. Under Phil Baker's guidance in 1991-1992, the church started periodic "Guest Sundays", a mix of dramatic arts and multimedia presentation designed to reach those outside the church, made plans for a television presentation called "Rhema Live" and introduced the slogan "the church for people who don't like church", which they maintain to the present day.

In 1997, Phil and Heather Baker established **Riverview Church** in the same building as the old Rhema fellowship, with a more ecumenical focus than its past incarnation, with a membership base that has grown consistently during the early 2000s. Phil was president of the Australian Christian Churches network and regularly wrote to newspapers and made media appearances representing the charismatic movement's point of view on a range of issues. The church also expanded to new campuses in Joondalup and Cockburn Central.

In June 2009, Phil Baker suffered a benign brain tumor, which had to be removed. The subsequent operation resulted in complications which meant his recovery time was increased greatly. In November 2010, Pastor Haydn

Nelson was named Senior Minister of Riverview Church. Under his leadership the church has continued to grow. The two suburban Riverview campuses were re-established as independent churches: Northreach Community Church in the north and The Red Door Community Church in the south.

World Harvest Centre

Suva, Fiji

4,000

It is the main headquarters of the Christian Mission Fellowship International located in Suva, the capital of the Fiji Islands

Pastor Suliasi Kurulo

Suliasi Kurulo, better known as "Pastor Suli," is the pastor of World Harvest Centre in Suva, Fiji Islands.

SOUTH AMERICA CHURCHES

There are 27 megachurches in 7 South American countries. Brazil heads the list with 14; Peru, Columbia, Argentina with 3 each; Chile 2; and Paraguay and Ecuador 1 each.

Campinas Central Church of the Nazarene
Campinas, Brazil

Lazaro Aguiar Valvassoura is the pastor of the Campinas Central Church of the Nazarene in Campinas, Brazil. Campinas Central is one of the largest Churches of the Nazarene congregations. He has been the pastor there since 1980.

In 1997 Point Loma Nazarene University awarded Valvassoura an honorary Doctor of Divinity degree.

Valvassoura withdrew his name for consideration for general superintendent at the 2005 General Assembly

On July 31, 1957, the first pioneer missionaries, Rev. Earl and Gladys Mosteller, arrived in Campinas, Brazil. In September of this year Charles and Roma Gates arrived to help with the work. In one of the visits that Rev. Mosteller made, a young man was converted in his own home. At the same time, contact was made with a Nazarene lady that had lived in Japan and had moved to Brazil.

The Church of the Nazarene officially started work in 1958, during the same time the Church of the Nazarene was celebrating its Golden Anniversary, 50 years of existence.

With the contacts previously mentioned along with others, the first service was held on the Wednesday after Easter Sunday, 1959, in the home of Elvin Stegmoller (a faithful Nazarene employed by the LeTourneau-Westinghouse Company, who had established business in Campinas). There were 19 people at this meeting and the attendance continued to grow until on May 31, there were 40 people present. At that time, Pastor Joaquin and his wife, citizens of Cape Verde, were living in Buenos Aires. They were invited to be the first Portuguese-speaking pastors of the new mission. From then on Rev. Lima has held important positions in the Brazilian work.

On November 1, 1959, Dr. G.B. Williamson, General Superintendent, visited Brazil and on this occasion organized the First Church of the Nazarene in Brazil with 15 charter members.

They rented a building and started services on November 1959. In the first service there were 150 in attendance.

A look at the statistics reveal that in 1961, after two years of work, there were 23 churches and preaching points and 110 members. Three churches were self-supporting. Eight Missionaries and five Brazilian workers took care of these works. On year later, the membership had grown to 156. One decade later, in 1979, there were 36 churches and preaching points, 21 Brazilian workers and 16 missionaries. Membership had grown to 828.

The reports from 1972 state that the membership of the Church of the Nazarene in Brazil had reached 1,184, but only one church was enjoying self-support. In August 1973 the mission celebrated its fourteenth year of work in the country. The extension of the work in 1973 covered three states, Minas Gerais, Río de Janeiro and Sao Paulo, plus the Federal District of Brasilia.

The city of Campinas, now the seat of the Church of the Nazarene in Brazil, also was the site of the Nazarene Theological School.

International Charismatic Mission
Bogota, Colombia
250,000

It is a Bogotá, Colombia based church founded in 1983 by César and Claudia Castellanos as a cell group with 8 people. As of 2008, the church had more than 250,000 members, organized into a structure of small cell groups. The church's teaching are titled the G12 Vision, which is based upon the mentoring of 12 disciples similar in method to Jesus. Castellanos stated that he was inspired to create the discipleship program after receiving a vision from God in 1983.[2]

Pastor Cesar Castellanos founder of "Misión Carismática Internacional" (MCI) in Bogota, Colombia started with only eight people in his living room. Through Pastor Cesar's fervent belief in God, MCI today has more than 200,000 members and more than 45,000 cells in the City of Bogota.

The revolutionary strategies that the Lord revealed to him for church multiplication are now known as the G12 Vision

or the Government of 12. The mission of Pastor Cesar and his wife Claudia who is also a senator of Colombia, is to fulfill God's command in Matthew 28:19 'to go and make disciples of all nations'. It is their desire that every believer will be equipped to become a leader of leaders.

It was conceived by Pastor César Castellanos in 1983 after Castellanos received a vision from God instructing him to implement this structure of cell groups of twelve. It was first modeled in his church in Bogotá, Colombia which has now grown up from an originally 8 members up to 200,000 members, composing of 45,000 cell groups.

Pastor César Castellanos developed the G12 strategy after visiting with Pastor David Yonggi Cho, who had successfully implemented a cell-group structure in the Yoido Full Gospel Church in South Korea. With about 1,000,000 members,

Yoido is the largest Protestant Christian congregation in the world.

Pastor César returned to his church, Misión Carismática Internacional in Bogotá, Colombia, with the revelation that he received from God while he was in South Korea — that God had given him a vision which would increase the number of Christian believers and help him to care for the growing numbers of people.

Aim of the G12 Vision

The aim of the G12 Vision is to form disciples with a Christ-like character who in turn will 'go and make disciples' as commanded by Jesus. Through prayer, encounters with God, teaching, support and encouragement, disciples are then encouraged to also make disciples. In both theory and example this process leads the church to grow exponentially, without losing accountability of Christian values due to the eventual size of the church.

G12 Methodology

The G12 Vision is based on the methodology used by Jesus to begin his ministry, when he chose the Twelve Apostles. Following his 40 days temptation in the desert, the first act of Jesus in his ministry was to form a group of 12 disciples, who were all men. (Mark 3:14). Additionally, in the book of Acts the first action taken by the 11 remaining disciples (Judas Iscariot having been instrumental in Jesus' eventual crucifixion and therefore no longer part of the group) was to re-establish a group of 12. Seeing fit not to leave it at 11, or allow 13, but rather to cast lots, which fell on Matthias, to fulfill the 12. Jesus of course included women in His group of disciples, Mary Magdalene and His own Mother for example but the men only are counted as Apostles. (Acts 1:26). It was only after the re-established as a 12, that the day of Pentecost came, although Jesus had already appeared to both men and women and many men and women were present, not just the 12 Apostles, when the Holy Spirit fell at Pentecost.

The G12 Vision is explained by Pastor Cesar in his self-published books, *Dream and you will Win the World*, and *Successful Leadership Through the Government of 12*.

Ladder of Success

"Ladder of Success" is used to describe the main steps of the G12 Vision.

- Win: Evangelism aiming to win people to a new belief in Christ.
- Consolidate: Bridging a convert to a disciple
- Disciple: Preparing the person for leadership
- Send: Making them a leader of leaders

G12 International Conference

An annual G12 International Conference is held in Bogotá, Colombia in January and is hosted by Misión Carismática Internacional church. The President of Colombia has frequently attended these events. Former President of Colombia (2002–2010) Álvaro Uribe attended in 2004, 2005, 2007, 2008, and 2009. In 2006, Senator Germán Vargas Lleras attended and in 2010, former Minister of

Defense and future President, Juan Manuel Santos spoke at the conference. At the 2012 conference Álvaro Uribe returned to thank the church and delegates for their prayers and support during his time in government. In 2013, former President Uribe and current President Santos attended the conference as special guests. Over the years, there have been many influential leaders and pastors attending the international conference; such as, Prophet Cindy Jacobs, Martin Smith of Delirious, Cece Winans, John Maxwell, and many more.

G12 Internationally

Many churches of all denominations around the world work with the G12 Vision. Conferences are held each year on every continent.

King of Kings

Buenos Aires, Argentina

20,000

CLAUDIO FREIDZON, born in Buenos Aires, Argentina in 1955, came to know the Lord at a very young age. Freidzon graduated from the River Plate Bible Institute of the Assemblies of God in 1977 and began pastoral work together with his wife Betty in Parque Chas, Buenos Aires. He served for seven years and finished his post-graduate studies in the Institute of Higher Ministerial Training of the Assemblies of God (ISUM) with a degree in Theology. In 1986, Freidzon founded the King of Kings Church in Argentina, which today has a weekly attendance of over 15,000 members.

Claudio Freidzon is the pastor of Rey de Reyes Church in Buenos Aires, Argentina which he began in 1986. He is the host of the TV program Rey de Reyes TV, bestselling author, and was among the first in South America to lead the way as an Evangelist with miracle services.

Claudio Freidzon first had a personal encounter with God when he was in an outdoor venue on the outskirts of Buenos Aires. This encounter sparked a desire to express the love of Christ to all those around him. In 1986 he founded the Church "King of Kings", which currently has over 20,000 members.

Six years later, Pastor Claudio Freidzon's personal quest led him to have another powerful encounter with the Holy Spirit, which revolutionized his life and ministry. Thousands of people from all over the world have come to his church for spiritual renewal. The Pastor has also participated in large crusades and conferences on five continents, personally ministering to more than two and a half million people. These crusades are characterized by the union of the pastors of each city, which has created a powerful movement of the Holy Spirit. There are beautiful testimonies of miracles and profound spiritual renewal from pastors and brothers of every place he visited.

Universal Church of the Kingdom of God

Brazil – 8,000,000

The **Universal Church of the Kingdom of God** (UCKG, from **Igreja Universal do Reino de Deus** [i'greʒe univeʁ'saw du 'ʁejnu dʒi 'dews]) is a Pentecostal Christian denomination with headquarters in the Temple of Solomon, in São Paulo, Brazil. It was founded on July 9, 1977 in Rio de Janeiro by Edir Macedo.

In 1999 it had 8 million members in Brazil, and had established temples in the United Kingdom and, since 1992, set up temples in Africa and in India, with a 1999 total of more than 12 million members worldwide. By 2013 UCKG had congregations in Brooklyn, New York City and other US locations.

The Church has frequently been accused of illegal activities and corruption, including money laundering, charlatanism, and witchcraft, and intolerance towards other religions. It has been subject to bans in several African counties, and was implicated in the murder in Britain of Victoria Climbié, only prayed for rather than protected and treated. There have been accusations that the Church extracts money from poor members for the benefit of its leaders.

Macedo converted to Evangelism at *Igreja Cristã de Nova Vida*, a Pentecostal church founded by the Canadian bishop

Walter Robert McAlister. In 1968 he met Soares, who also joined. Macedo wanted to become a minister of that church, but was not accepted by its leaders, and decided to change to another denomination. Soares became interested in another church, called *Casa da Bênção*, and invited Macedo. In that new church they saw for the first time the boldness in possession and deliverance of demons, but only Soares was consecrated as a pastor.

Edir Macedo still wanted to start his ministry; in 1975 Soares and another pastor invited him to inaugurate the Cruzada do Caminho Eterno, which was a kind of embryo of the Universal Church. The services were held in some cinemas they rented for a few hours. To increase the number of members Macedo began to preach in a gazebo at the main square of the Méier neighborhood.

In 1977 Macedo rented the building of a former funeral home, officially the first temple of the Universal Church of the Kingdom of God, and also the beginning of the dispute between its founders Macedo and Soares, because Soares thought the rent was too high.

In 1980 Macedo went to New York state to start the ministry in the United States, but soon returned to Brazil to solve administrative problems with Soares. Some of Macedo's principles clashed with those of Soares, such as, according to Macedo, the hiring of pastors from other denominations while Macedo was planning a completely fresh denomination, financial management, the centralization of the image of the "Missionary R. R. Soares". They decided to call a vote for the leadership among the 15 pastors UCKG had at the time; Macedo won by twelve votes to three.

In 1989 Macedo and the Church purchased Rede Record, which by 2013 was Brazil's second-largest television network. In 2009 the Workers' Party (PT) government in Brazil bought advertising from Rede Record, which it had formerly limited to Catholic publications, in new venues, and paid for public service messages in UCKG media outlets.

The church follows prosperity theology, asserting that faith and commitment to a church are rewarded with wealth. And in the late 1990s started trying to change its image of being associated with only the poorest people. In 1998 Macedo appointed his nephew Marcelo Crivella as Bishop. Crivella said, "We want to win the middle class."[3] In 1992, Crivella began a mission in Africa, resulting in the creation of multiple UCKG temples. Crivella returned to Brazil in 1998, and was given a four-bedroom condominium in an exclusive development, where Macedo also lives. He is married to Sylvia Jane, with three children who attend a Methodist school in Río de Janeiro.

The church's influence

According to Forbes magazine, as of 2015 UCKG's founder Edir Macedo had a personal fortune estimated at US$1.1 billion, largely from his ownership of Rede Record, the second largest broadcaster in Brazil. The church's continuing growth, and controversies since Macedo purchased Rede Record attracted frequent media attention. In addition, claims against the church and government efforts related to other investigations have caused review of its operations. In 2013 Macedo acquired a 49% stake in privately held bank Banco Renner, with among the highest interest rates in Brazil; the source of funding to buy the bank is unclear, and some reports alleged that he used church funds.

Reports in 2009 from a Brazilian governmental investigation of money laundering estimated that the Church received R$1.4 billion per year in tithes, collected in 4,500 temples in 1,500 cities in Brazil. From 2003 to 2008, deposits for the Universal Church of the Kingdom God in Brazil reached R$3.9 billion.

Doctrines

Most UCKG doctrines are the same as most conservative Evangelical-Pentecostal doctrines. Specific doctrines include belief:

- That the baptism of the Holy Spirit empowers believers for service and endows them with supernatural gifts.
- That ministries of apostle, prophet, evangelist, pastor, and teacher are divinely ordained.
- That Jesus Christ appointed two ordinances to be observed as acts of obedience:
  - immersion of the believer in water (baptism)
  - The Lord's Supper, symbolic of consuming the body and blood of Jesus, in remembrance of his sacrifice and in the expectation that he will return.
- In divine healing as described in the Christian Bible. The translation recommended by the UCKG is the

1982 New King James Bible (NKJB; different from the original King James Bible, KJB); they say "it is the most true to the original we've found so far. Also be aware of the Jehovah's Witness version."

- That people can be sanctified (become holy during their lifetime.
- The UCKG does not believe that the sacrifice of Jesus Christ is sufficient enough to work in the congregant's life today, therefore they teach that a member of the church has to 'sacrifice' what he depends on to God through the church (for example, all of their income, savings, etc.) twice a year, they commonly refer this as the "Campaign of Israel."

Lagoinha Baptist Church

Brazil

70,000

(Igreja Batista da Lagoinha) is a Christian Pentecostal megachurch located in Belo Horizonte, Minas Gerais in Brazil. Márcio Valadão is the current senior pastor of the church and has about 70,000 members. The main Temple but holds about 8.000 seats. The church has many services during a Sunday. Additionally specific services during the week, e.g. for families, for businesses, a prophetic services, and some services for teenagers and young adults. It is one of the best-known evangelical churches in Brazil. The church became known through the ministry of praise Diante do Trono, which is one of the ministries of the church. Some of the main services are broadcoasted live via the Internet and also via their on TV and radio station Rede Super.

In 2011 it was announced the construction of the new temple of Lagoinha Church will involve about 25.000 people sitting.

History

Lagoinha Church was founded by José Rego on December 20, 1957. It is the sixth Baptist Church in Belo Horizonte, became known as Lagoinha Baptist Church. The church also has a television network titled Rede Super.

Since 2010 the Lagoinha Baptist Church is a partner of Gateway Church of the United States.

Senior Pastor

On May 15, 1958 Pastor José Rego Nascimento arrives in the church bringing Pentecostal guidance to Lagoinha Church. On July 31, 1972 the current pastor Márcio Valadão assumed the presidency of the church.

This ministry holds church services and other events in English and in Spanish every Sunday. Foreigners are very welcome. Services in other languages are planned.

On January 31, 1998 the Diante do Trono, ministry led by Ana Paula Valadão, daughter of the pastor Márcio Valadão, recorded his first album titled "Diante do Trono" in Lagoinha Church to collect funds for missionary work in India. The album sold a lot, and came the worship ministry Diante do Trono which became the biggest worship ministry in Latin America, emerged from Lagoinha Church. It was from this that the Lagoinha Church began to be recognized.

Several ministries and big names came from Lagoinha Church. The Lagoinha Church has several projects like CTMDT and the Fábrica de Artes, which is a partnership with Gateway Church of the United States.[

On July 7, 2013 opened one Lagoinha Church, in Niterói, in Rio de Janeiro by pastors Felippe and Mariana Valadão. In celebration of one year of the Lagoinha Church in Niterói, opened a new temple which holds about 4,500 people and has 10,000.

Ten Richest Pastors

You Won't Believe Are Millionaires

A few years ago no one would have thought that being a pastor could be a ticket to fortune and wealth, but times have changed. Below is a list of 10 Richest Pastors who are raking in megabucks as they spread the word.

1. David Oyedepo $150 Million

Being a cleric has never been so profitable ask Nigerian pastor David Oyedepo whose net worth sits at $150 million. Oyedepo also known as "papa" is the founder of Living Faith Church World Wide. The man Of God is not shy of splurging

his wealth on the good life. He owns a Rolls-Royce Phantom and a fleet of private jets.

2. Benny Hinn $42 Million

The American Evangelist has been spreading the word since 1983 when he established the Orlando Christian Center. Hinn's popularity has continued to soar through the years, which has seen him become one of the richest pastors with a net worth of $42 Million. His ability to "cure" terminal illnesses such as cancer has, however, been a source of controversy.

3. Joel Osteen $40 Million

Joel's high-watt charisma has endeared audiences all over the world. He is the senior pastor of Lakewood Church, which was founded by his late father John Osteen. Today, Lakewood stands as the largest and fastest growing church in America. With over 40,000 attendees every week, the Church undoubtedly brings in thousands. But Joel's appeal transcends the altar; he is also a bestselling author. His net worth stands at $40 million.

4. Chris Oyakhilome $30-50 Million

Oyakhilome is yet another Nigerian Pastor who is making some good money from the church ministry. He is the man behind Christ Embassy, a church and mission group with offices in United Kingdom, USA, and South Africa. Forbes estimates Pastor Chris' net worth to be between $30-50 million.

5. Creflo Dollar $27 Million

His name screams money, and he does have a lot of it. Pastor Dollar is one of the prominent African-American pastors in the USA. His World Changers International commands a huge following with 30,000 followers stemming from the Atlanta region alone. His net worth is estimated at $27 million, but it could be more. He is known to be quite privy when it comes to his financial assets.

6. Billy Graham $25 Million

Graham is the longest serving Evangelical Pastor on our list with his ministry dating back to the 1940s. His spiritual allure has seen him become the advisor of several presidents including Lyndon Johnson. The 95 year old pastor whose net worth stands at $25 million remains one of the most revered clerics of the 20th century.

7. Rick Warren $25 Million

 Besides being the pastor of the eighth largest church in the USA (Saddleback Church), Rick has also authored numerous Christian books which have sold millions of copies. While some of the pastors on our list live multi-million dollar lifestyles, Rick's lifestyle is considerably down to earth. He admittedly gives away 90% of his income and lives off 10%. He is worth $25 Million.

8. T.D Jakes $18 Million

This Charismatic Bishop has managed to capture the hearts of many Christians. He is the founder and chief pastor of The Potter's House which boasts of having 30,000 members. His net worth of $18 million largely stems from his ministry, but besides being a fiery Bishop, he is also an author and an actor.

9. Temitope Joshua $15 Million

Pastor Temitope has made a name for himself as one of the most charitable Nigerian Evangelists. When he founded The Synagogue Church Of All Nations, he never imagined his net worth would one day sum up to $15 million. He only had a handful of followers for the first few months, but today more than 15,000 members turn up for his Sunday service.

10. Matthew Ashimolowo $6-10 Million

Matthew had been a Muslim until the age of 22 when he converted to Christianity after his father's death. He attended Bible School and developed a keen interest in the religion. Today, he is the senior pastor of Kingsway International Christian Centre. His net worth which is estimated at $6-10 million has been bolstered by documentaries from his media company and the sale of Christian literature.

www.ingramcontent.com/pod-product-compliance
Lightning Source LLC
Chambersburg PA
CBHW060919040426

42445CB00011B/697